Social Phobia

CLINICAL APPLICATION OF EVIDENCE-BASED PSYCHOTHERAPY

A Series of Books Edited By

William C. Sanderson

In response to the demands of the new health care environment, there is a movement in psychology (and in all of health care) toward defining empirically supported treatment approaches (i.e., treatments that have been shown to be effective in controlled research studies). The future demands of psychotherapy are becoming clear. In response to pressures from managed care organizations and various practice guidelines, clinicians will be required to implement evidence-based, symptom-focused treatments.

Fortunately, such treatments exist for a variety of the most commonly encountered disorders. However, it has been extremely difficult to disseminate these treatments from clinical research centers, where the treatments are typically developed, to practitioners. More often than not, the level of detail in treatment protocols used in research studies is insufficient to teach a clinician to implement the treatment.

This series, *Clinical Application of Evidence-Based Psychotherapy*, will address this issue. For each disorder covered, empirically supported psychological procedures will be identified. Then, an intensive, step-by-step, session-by-session treatment application will be provided. A detailed clinical vignette will be woven throughout, including session transcripts.

All books in this series are written by experienced clinicians who have applied the treatments to a wide variety of patients, and have supervised and taught other clinicians how to apply them.

Social Phobia:
Clinical Application of Evidence-Based Psychotherapy
Ronald Rapee and William C. Sanderson

Overcoming Shyness and Social Phobia:
A Step-by-Step Guide
Ronald Rapee

Specific Phobias:
Clinical Applications of Evidence-Based Psychotherapy
Timothy J. Bruce and William C. Sanderson

Cognitive-Behavioral Treatment of Depression
Janet S. Klosko and William C. Sanderson

Social Phobia

CLINICAL APPLICATION
OF
EVIDENCE-BASED PSYCHOTHERAPY

Ronald M. Rapee, Ph.D.

William C. Sanderson, Ph.D.

JASON ARONSON INC.
Northvale, New Jersey
London

This book was set in 12 pt. Fairfield Light by Alpha Graphics of Pittsfield, New Hampshire and printed and bound by Book-mart Press, Inc. of North Bergen, New Jersey.

Library of Congress Cataloging-in-Publication Data
Rapee, Ronald M.
    Social phobia : clinical application of evidence-based
psychotherapy / Ronald M. Rapee, William C. Sanderson.
        p.   cm.
    Includes bibliographical references and index.
    ISBN 0-7657-0004-2 (alk. paper)
    1. Social phobia—Treatment.   I. Sanderson, William C.
II. Title.
RC552.S62R36   1997
616.85'225—dc21   97-19446

Printed in the United States of America on acid-free paper. Jason Aronson Inc. offers books and cassettes. For information and catalog write to Jason Aronson Inc., 230 Livingston Street, Northvale, New Jersey 07647-1731. Or visit our website: http://www.aronson.com

✥ Contents ✥

ॐ Introduction ॐ

There is a perception among the public that "being shy" is a common and normal part of a person's character that therefore does not require help and indeed probably cannot be changed. While parts of this conception are true—social fears are certainly common and they are definitely not abnormal in any major sense of the word—the rest of the statement is incorrect. Recent evidence clearly shows that social anxiety can have a tremendous debilitating and restricting effect on an individual's life. One of the most famous studies in this area (Caspi et al. 1988) showed that shy youngsters tended to still be shy thirty years later and that this shyness interfered with relationships, career, and family life. A more recent study (Norton et al. 1996) also demonstrated that social phobia can produce more interference in a person's life than panic disorder, affecting relationships, employment, and drug use. In addition, there is considerable evidence that treatment programs for social phobia can be highly effective in producing change and in markedly reducing life interference.

Media attention and professional interest in social phobia have increased in recent years. As a result, you are likely to find increased numbers of clients seeking treatment for social fears. The good news, as mentioned above, is that tried and tested treatment programs do exist. This book provides a detailed guide on how to approach clients with social phobia. The components of the program are based on empirically validated techniques and the chapters are organized to provide a logically structured program. Every client and therapist will have individual needs. Therefore, the components of the program are set out in chapters rather than session by session. This allows you to be flexible with respect to the length of treatment. Where you are working within the confines of eight sessions, each chapter can form the basis of a new session. On the other hand, if time allows, you may wish to spend several sessions on one component. Finally, the book was written largely from the perspective of treatment with an individual client, but it can just as easily be applied to a group format.

There is also a companion book that was written with the current program in mind (Rapee 1998). This is a client book that contains all of the principles, instructions, and monitoring forms from this program in a format that can be used directly with clients. Ideally, clients should have a copy of the client book so that they can work through it together with their therapist. This will save repetition and copying of monitoring forms, and will help to make the whole process more efficient, especially when you are trying to make the treatment process as streamlined as possible.

Introduction to Social Phobia

1

Diagnosis and Assessment of Social Phobia

A WORD ABOUT TERMINOLOGY

Terms such as *shyness, social phobia, social anxiety, heterosocial dating anxiety, love shyness,* and many others have all been used to describe largely similar problems. While there is not space here to enter into a discussion of the similarities and differences, we can simply say that experimental evidence has failed to find major differences between clinical populations defined as socially phobic and non-clinical populations who describe themselves as "shy" (Turner et al. 1990). Therefore, throughout this book, we will use these terms interchangeably. In general, we will use terms such as *social anxiety* or *shyness* when describing direct instructions to clients because these terms are acceptable to most lay people. However, the terms you personally use should be a decision based on your own beliefs and the beliefs of your client.

DIAGNOSTIC ISSUES

Criteria

Social phobia simply refers to a fear of social situations, that is, situations that involve social interaction or the possibility of evaluation by another. The specific diagnostic criteria, as outlined in the *DSM-IV*, are listed in Table 1–1.

People with social phobia fear and often avoid a wide variety of social/evaluative situations. These include dating, meeting new people, attending or speaking up at meetings, entering a room full of people, or speaking to authority figures, to list a few. Basically, any situation where the person is the focus of others' attention may be potentially difficult. There are also several other types of situations that can fit this profile. These include speaking in public, performing in front of others (e.g., acting, singing), being assertive, and facing test situations. While people with these specific problems may not always meet full criteria for social phobia (although they often

Table 1–1. Diagnostic criteria for social phobia.

SOCIAL PHOBIA (SOCIAL ANXIETY DISORDER)

A. Marked persistent fear of social or performance situations in which one is exposed to unfamiliar people or possible scrutiny by others. Individual fears that s/he will act in a way (or show anxiety symptoms) that are embarrassing or humiliating.
B. Exposure to the feared situation provokes anxiety.
C. Person recognizes that the fear is excessive or unreasonable.
D. Feared social situations are avoided or endured with dread.
E. Interferes significantly with person's life.
F. Duration at least 6 months if under 18 years.
G. Fear is not due to direct physiological effects of a substance, or general medical condition.
H. If a general medical condition exists, fear is unrelated to it.

Specify generalized type if fear includes most social situations.

Reprinted with permission from the *Diagnostic and Statistical Manual of Mental Disorders, Fourth Edition*. Copyright © 1994 American Psychiatric Association.

do), the problems are certainly extremely similar and will respond well to the program outlined in this book. Finally, there exists one other type of person with social phobia who should not be overlooked. Some individuals have specific fears of performing a particular action in front of others. The most common fears include writing, eating, drinking, working, or urinating (in a public restroom) in front of others. These difficulties are often part of a more general picture of social phobia but can sometimes exist as isolated problems. In almost all cases, people with these problems will meet criteria for social phobia, sometimes being referred to as having specific or nongeneralized social phobia. They will also respond well to the procedures outlined in this book.

The central issue in social phobia has been pointed out by several authors as being a fear of negative evaluation. People with social fears will often report concerns that others will laugh at them, think they are stupid, or in some way think badly of them. This is often totally independent of their own views of themselves. People with social phobia can have a very healthy view of their own abilities. They do not necessarily think badly of themselves but rather believe that others will think badly of them. Of course, sometimes, poor self-esteem does form a part of the picture, in which case there is an additional problem to deal with. Usually, when people have low self-esteem in addition to their social fears, they are also likely to experience low mood or depression, a point that will be discussed more in the next section.

Comorbidity

Like any disorder, social phobia frequently co-occurs with other disorders (Sanderson et al. 1990). In such instances, there may be an impact on treatment. In all cases, a decision needs to be made as to what is the principal or main diagnosis and what are additional or secondary diagnoses (cf. Wetzler and Sanderson 1997). Sometimes certain problems must be dealt with before treatment for social

phobia can commence. For example, if a client is psychotically para-
noid, this would generally need to be dealt with before treatment
for social phobia begins. However, in other cases, the decision as to
which is the more important or pressing problem can be made by
your client. If he wishes to work on social fears as a priority, this
program can be instituted as a first step. If he has other issues to
deal with earlier, this program can be instituted at a later time.

Anxiety Disorders

The most frequent comorbidity for social phobia is with other anxiety disorders. This generally has little impact on treatment outcome
and it is usually best to simply address the disorder that is most
important to the client's life. The treatment of all anxiety disorders
basically follows similar lines and you will often find that you can
address treatment for more than one anxiety disorder simultaneously.

Mood Disorders

It is also not uncommon for people with social phobia to be depressed. They often have fewer friends and less social support than
others and naturally this can increase the risk for depression. In
addition, some people with social phobia will have fundamentally
poor self-esteem so that not only do they believe others will think
badly of them, but they think the negative evaluation is accurate and
they are indeed hopeless.

Whether or not the depressed mood meets full criteria for a disorder, its presence may still affect treatment outcome. You will need
to decide whether the mood disturbance is severe enough to interfere with treatment for the social fears. In particular, low mood is
likely to result in low motivation and hopelessness about getting
better. However, if it appears that the individual is sufficiently
motivated to commence treatment addressing the social fears, you
will often find that mood and motivation begin to improve when treat-

ment gains begin to become evident. Naturally, if suicidal ideation is present, it will need to be monitored and may have to be addressed first.

Substance Abuse

A certain proportion of people with social phobia will also abuse drugs, most commonly alcohol (Schneier et al. 1992). In fact, a sizeable proportion of people at alcohol detoxification centers are found to meet criteria for social phobia or avoidant personality disorder (Stravinsky et al. 1986). When alcohol abuse occurs, it most commonly follows the onset of social phobia and is used as a form of self-medication. Therefore, conceptually, the social phobia is maintaining the alcohol abuse and will need to be dealt with in order to reduce reliance on the drug. Unfortunately, when substance abuse becomes severe and chronic, it can develop a life of its own and may require independent treatment, including detoxification.

The primary decision here is whether the substance abuse is so severe that it is interfering with cognitive processing capacity, or if the client is physically dependent on the alcohol. If this is the case (and especially if the client is drinking before sessions), the alcohol problem will need to be dealt with first. If this is not the case, you will often find that as treatment for the social phobia progresses and he is able to substitute skills learned in treatment for the substance in order to manage anxiety, you can begin to encourage the client to gradually reduce his reliance on the substance.

Personality Disorders

The most common personality disorder accompanying social phobia is avoidant personality disorder. Some studies have estimated that over 60 percent of people with generalized social phobia will meet criteria for avoidant personality disorder (Herbert et al. 1992). However, to a large extent this is a function of semantic problems with

the *DSM*. The diagnostic criteria for avoidant personality disorder
are very similar to those for social phobia, so it is not surprising that
there is considerable overlap. In any case, people who meet additional criteria for avoidant personality disorder can be treated in much
the same way as those who only meet criteria for social phobia. Treatment may be more difficult, slower, and longer for clients with
avoidant personality disorder because it is a more chronic and per-
vasive disorder. However, the procedures described in this book will
be of value in addressing the basic psychopathology.

Other personality disorders may co-occur with social phobia just
as they might with any Axis I disorder. The common folklore is that
when personality disorders exist, treatment outcome will be compromised. However, empirical evidence on this issue is mixed. Specific studies of the effect of personality disorders on treatment outcome for social phobia have shown both no effect (Brown et al. 1995)
and some lessening of treatment effects (Feske and Chambless
1995). However, even in studies in which treatment outcome is
shown to be compromised by the presence of additional Axis II disorders, the effects are not large and most clients are still able to make
substantial progress.

FACTS AND FIGURES

Prevalence

Prevalence figures are often relatively unreliable because of problems of definition. As a result figures for the frequency of social fears
vary considerably. The NIMH-funded Epidemiological Catchment
Area Study has recently indicated a lifetime prevalence for social
phobia of around 13 percent (Kessler et al. 1994). On the other hand,
a study conducted in New Zealand using *DSM-III* criteria estimated
a lifetime prevalence for social phobia of only 3 percent (Wells et al.
1989). From a different perspective, Philip Zimbardo and colleagues
(1974) conducted a less rigorous study many years ago in which they

asked university students how many would describe themselves as shy. A whopping 40 percent placed themselves in this category. Thus, it would appear that by even the most conservative estimates, millions of individuals suffer impairment as a result of social anxiety.

Age

The typical age of onset for social phobia is also problematic. Retrospective studies of adults with social phobia typically indicate a mean age of onset around the mid- to late teens. However, children as young as 8 often meet criteria for social phobia and many adults report being shy all of their lives. Most probably, a basic shyness is part of a person's life virtually from birth. However, this characteristic is more likely to begin to be a problem for people when they reach their teens and there is increased pressure to socialize (Rapee 1995).

People with social phobia may present for treatment at any age. The average age of presentation seems to be around the 30s, which is a little later than panic disorder but earlier than generalized anxiety disorder. However, we have treated people from ages 7 to 65. Importantly, age does not seem to predict response to treatment.

Gender Distribution

Gender is another statistic with mixed results, depending on where the data come from. Epidemiological and survey studies indicate more social fears in females and more females meeting criteria for social phobia. In contrast, treatment studies typically report equal numbers of males and females, and sometimes even more males. It appears that while females report more social fears than males (as for all anxiety disorders), social phobia may result in greater life interference for males (e.g., traditional gender roles require that males take the proactive stance with respect to dating) and therefore they are more likely to present for treatment (Rapee 1995).

Life Interference

Social phobia can have a major impact on a person's life. People with social phobia are known to have less social contacts than others, are less likely to be married, have more restricted career choices, and utilize more health and welfare services (Rapee 1995). Even in mild cases there can be many subtle restraints in a sufferer's life. Social life can be restricted, promotions can be foregone, and family life can be filled with friction. The idea held by many people that being shy is a part of a person's personality that should just be accepted clearly does not take into account the many lost opportunities caused by this problem.

THE ASSESSMENT OF SOCIAL PHOBIA

Initial Interview

People with social phobia may come to you with a wide variety of presenting problems. These may include shyness, performance fears, public speaking fear, dating anxiety, loneliness, job difficulties, and many others. Aside from the usual aims of any initial interview (rapport building, provision of motivation and hope, basic information, etc.), you will need to answer two main questions: (1) Does the person have social phobia? (2) Is social phobia the primary or most pressing problem?

The first question is obviously more important. You will need to conduct a standard interview to determine whether the person meets the criteria described earlier for social phobia. Of course, a program along the lines of the current one may be appropriate even if the person does not meet full technical criteria for social phobia as outlined in the *DSM-IV*, but still has a basic social concern mediated by a fear of negative evaluation. If you are unused to diagnostic interviews or are unsure of the direction to go, there are several structured interviews available (e.g. the Anxiety Disorders Interview Schedule—[Di Nardo et al. 1993]) that will provide detailed questions to assist you in making a correct diagnosis. Some key questions are:

- Do you ever worry that other people will in some way judge you negatively or think badly of you?
- Are there any situations or activities that you avoid or would like to avoid because you worry about what people will think of you?
- What sorts of situations or activities do you avoid or try to avoid and what sorts of things do you worry about if you have to enter those situations?
- In what ways does your worry about what people think of you stop you from doing things that are important?

It is usually a good idea to begin by asking people about the types of situations that make them anxious. Language can sometimes be an issue. Some people will not use the word "anxiety" to describe their social concerns but may use words such as "embarrassed" or "uncomfortable." Once you have a list of feared situations, this will give you a good idea of whether they are typical of people with social phobia. Some of the most common situations feared by people with social phobia include public speaking, going on dates, entering rooms where people are already seated, crowded situations (e.g., public transport, lecture halls, theaters), assertiveness situations, and situations that attract attention (e.g., wearing bright clothes, performing in front of others, telling jokes). Nevertheless, it is still important to go back and determine *why* the person becomes anxious in these situations. If this is a difficult question, you may want to prompt the person by asking about the types of thoughts he has in such situations. Importantly, you are looking for some type of concern with *negative evaluation* (e.g., "they will laugh at me," "they will think I look stupid," "they won't like me," etc.). Several diagnostic groups may share fears of particular situations and it is only the underlying belief or motivation for the fear that will distinguish them. For example, an individual who fears crowds may do so out of concern that the crowd will turn on him (paranoia?), a fear that he will have a panic attack and not be able to escape (agoraphobia?), a fear that he will not be able to breathe (claustrophobia?), or a fear that people will think he looks funny (social phobia?). Simply determining that the person fears crowds, then, is not diagnostic of social phobia. Evaluating the underlying beliefs associated with the fear is essential.

Obviously there is much more information that needs to be obtained and that will be important in determining the direction of treatment. We will not discuss here the specifics of initial interviews, as most good introductory therapy books cover this topic. However, it is essential to obtain explicit detail. This is particularly relevant to the feared situations. You need to ask about the parameters that influence the degree of fear, discomfort or embarrassment. For example, does the gender or size of the audience or the formality of the situation affect the level of anxiety experienced? If so, why does the client feel that way? You should also obtain full details of the effects of the situation on the person. For example, what are his feelings (frightened, embarrassed), thoughts ("others think I'm ugly"), physical reactions (racing heart, trembling, blushing), and behavioral reactions (escaping from the situation, avoiding saying too much, avoiding eye contact)? Finally, the breadth of the problem needs to be carefully explored. Many people will present with a relatively specific problem, such as a fear of public presentations leading to restricted work opportunities, and will initially or superficially deny any additional restrictions caused by social concerns. However, detailed probing may well reveal some degree of restriction in other areas of life, perhaps something like always being the quiet one in a group. While we are not saying that treatment should be specifically aimed at areas that the client does not see as important, it is often very useful in the latter part of treatment to have a complete knowledge of the person's limitations. For example, practice of treatment techniques in these lesser situations can be very valuable for improving performance in the main situation and is also helpful in preventing relapse.

Once you have determined that the client has socially mediated concerns, you will need to identify other difficulties the person may have. As described above, comorbidity is common. If comorbid conditions are identified, you will need to determine whether social anxiety is the main problem or the one most appropriate for initial focus. In most cases this will be fairly obvious, either due to practical considerations (severe alcohol abuse, for example, would require addressing first) or from the way in which the client has described the problems (the client presents with comorbid depression but the focus of depression appears to be loneliness, a consequence of the client's social phobia). In other cases, it is quite appropriate to leave the ultimate decision up to the client. You can simply summarize each of the areas of difficulty as you have heard them and then ask the client to decide which area he would first like to address. Of course, as we mentioned earlier, in many cases several similar problems can be addressed simultaneously (cf Sanderson and McGinn 1997).

QUESTIONNAIRE MEASURES

Questionnaires are not generally considered a vital part of clinical practice, but they can play a useful role, both to expand or support the information obtained at interview and to provide a means of evaluating treatment progress. There are several measures of direct relevance to social phobia. Some of the more widely used and useful ones are as follows.

1. *Fear of Negative Evaluation Scale*: This is an early measure developed by Watson and Friend (1969) using nonclinical populations. Its main drawbacks are the use of many double negatives, making comprehension difficult, and the True/False format, which frustrates some clients. It is, however, probably

the most widely used measure and has been used frequently
with clinical populations so that norms do exist (see Heimberg
et al. 1988). It is also one of the only measures that assesses
the underlying concept in social phobia: the concern over negative evaluation. There is also a brief version of this scale that
contains only twelve items but still has good psychometric
properties (Leary 1983).

2. *The Social Phobia and Anxiety Inventory*: This is a measure
developed by Turner and colleagues (1989) primarily for use
with clinical social phobic populations. It is focused mainly on
feared situations and is a relatively long measure. However, it
is very comprehensive and provides a thorough coverage of the
client's social fears.

3. *The Albany Panic and Phobia Scale*: This measure was developed by Rapee and colleagues (1994) in order to provide a brief
assessment of feared situations relevant to several anxiety disorders. Its three subscales measure social fears, interoceptive
fears, and agoraphobic fears. The main advantage of this scale
is that it can provide a quick assessment of three major areas
of concern to anxious individuals. See Table 1–2.

4. *The Beck Anxiety Inventory and Beck Depression Inventory*:
These scales were both developed by Beck and colleagues
(1961, 1989) to provide broad measures of general anxiety and
depression/dysphoria. For people with social phobia they can
be very useful as quick, broad measures of general mood. The
BDI is especially important in order to keep a check on depression levels throughout treatment for clients for whom this is a
problem. In addition, the BDI contains one item on suicidal
ideation that can serve as a simple screen.

5. *Michigan Alcoholism Screening Test (short form)*: This measure
is a thirteen-item version of the original MAST and provides a
quick and simple screen for alcohol abuse (Selzer et al. 1975).
It can be useful to identify those clients for whom you may need
to keep track of alcohol issues.

Table 1–2. Albany Panic and Phobia Questionnaire (APPQ)

Name:_____   Date:_____

Using the following scale, please rate the *amount of fear* that you think you would experience in each of the situations listed below if they were to occur *in the next week*. Try to imagine yourself actually doing each activity and how you would feel.

Fear Scale

0——1———2——3———4———5———6———7———8
| no | slight | moderate | marked | extreme |
| fear | fear | fear | fear | fear |

1. Talking to people _____
2. Going through a car wash _____
3. Playing vigorous sport on a hot day _____
4. Blowing up an airbed quickly _____
5. Eating in front of others _____
6. Hiking on a hot day _____
7. Getting gas at a dentist _____
8. Interrupting a meeting _____
9. Giving a speech _____
10. Exercising vigorously alone _____
11. Going long distances from home alone _____
12. Introducing yourself to groups _____
13. Walking alone in isolated areas _____
14. Driving on highways _____
15. Wearing striking clothes _____
16. Possibility of getting lost _____
17. Drinking a strong cup of coffee _____
18. Sitting in the center of a cinema _____
19. Running up stairs _____
20. Riding on a subway _____
21. Speaking on the telephone _____
22. Meeting strangers _____
23. Writing in front of others _____
24. Entering a room full of people _____
25. Staying overnight away from home _____
26. Feeling the effects of alcohol _____
27. Going over a long, low bridge _____

Albany Panic and Phobia Scale. From Assessment instrument for panic disorder that includes fear of sensation-producing activities: The Albany Panic and Phobia Questionnaire, in *Anxiety*. Copyright © 1994 by John Wiley & Sons, Inc. Used with permission.

There are several more specific measures in existence assessing areas such as public speaking fears (Paul 1966), test anxiety (Suinn 1969), and unassertiveness (Rathus 1973).

SOCIAL PERFORMANCE

For some clients it may also be necessary to assess for deficits in social performance. In most cases this can be directly observed during the initial interview and the first few sessions. You may want to keep detailed notes on observed deficits such as lack of eye contact, poor voice tone, long pauses, and so on, as well as your reactions to these deficits in order to provide later feedback (see Chapter 9). If you would like to conduct a more formal assessment, it is often a good idea to set up a role play, either playing the "other" yourself or using a colleague in this role, making sure you have complete, preferably written, consent from the client. The role play can be about any social interaction situation, but is most useful if focused on one that the client identifies as especially difficult. It need only be five to ten minutes long and, ideally, should be videotaped for later feedback (see Chapter 9).

2

Understanding Social Phobia and Treatment Rationale

ORIGINS

Not a great deal is known about the origins of social phobia. This type of research is difficult to conduct and it is difficult to control for all variables. Nevertheless, there are a number of factors that are hypothesized to be responsible for the development of social phobia and that do have some empirical support. We will briefly describe these here. The reader is referred to Hudson and Rapee (in press) for a more complete discussion.

Genetic Factors

There is almost certainly a genetic basis to social phobia. However, few properly controlled studies support the argument that there is a specific genetic component to social fears. Rather, what seems to be inherited is what some authors have referred to as "the general neurotic syndrome" (Andrews 1996). In other words, the genetic component of social phobia is one that is general to all of the anxiety disorders. The channeling of this genetic predisposition into a specific disorder (social phobia) most probably occurs at the environmental level.

Childrearing Factors

There is considerable evidence that people who are socially phobic recall their parents as overprotective and possibly also as rejecting. Some (considerably less) evidence suggests that this recall may be real, that is, social phobics seem to have parents who control and protect them from life's experiences more than do nonanxious subjects (see Rapee 1997 for a review).

Family Socialization

There is also evidence that the families of people with social phobia engage in less social acitivity than do others. If this is true, it would suggest that shy children are exposed to fewer social experiences and also observe less social interaction by their families.

Other Life Events

Finally, there is some evidence that a number of other life events may distinguish shy children from others. Some studies have found that shy children are more likely to be the first born in a family, are more likely to have several serious illnesses while growing up, are more likely to be socially isolated, and are more likely to report specific severely embarrassing events (such as being laughed at by the entire class). Whether these events are causal in the development of social phobia is hard to say at this stage (Hudson and Rapee in press).

MAINTENANCE

Several models of the maintenance of social phobia have been proposed over recent years. Most share a number of basic similarities, although they may differ in terms of emphases. In order to place the forthcoming treatment into a theoretical perspective, we will briefly describe one recent model of social phobia (Rapee and Heimberg 1997). A schematic of the model is presented in Figure 2–1.

The model describes what happens when a person with social phobia enters an evaluative situation. The individual immediately generates a mental representation of how she presumably appears to the audience. This mental representation is made up of prior knowledge of the individual's general appearance together with

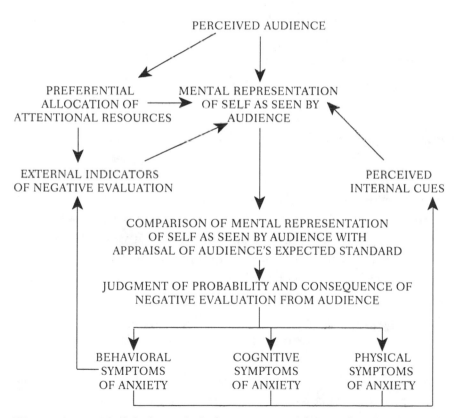

Figure 2–1. Model of social phobia. Reprinted from *Behaviour Research and Therapy*, 1997. Copyright by and with permission from Elsevier Science Ltd, The Boulevard, Langford Lane, Kidlington 0X5 1GB, UK.

momentary adjustments (for example, how her hair might look if she has just entered from a windy street). Most important, the mental representation of the person's appearance to others is not some sort of accurate mental photo. Rather, it is most likely a distorted image focusing primarily on the most salient aspects (to her) of her appearance. For example, if the person is worried about blushing and feels an increase in her facial heat, she might have an image of herself as a large red balloon. Or if the person has an ongoing concern about her ears sticking out, she might regularly have an image of two large, prominent ears. The mental representation of how one appears to others will also change from moment to moment in a situation based on both feedback from outside (audience cues) and feedback from inside (physical symptoms, thoughts, behavior). Presumably, people with social phobia will have an inaccurate initial image of their appearance and will receive feedback that they distort and exaggerate.

When a social phobic person enters an evaluative situation, she instantly allocates a large proportion of her attention in two directions. First, she focuses extensively on the mental representation of how she appears to others, in particular, on the salient parts of the representation, such as a scar on her face or awkward movements. Second, the social phobic will pay attention to any possible negative cues from the audience. Whereas most people will scan an audience for either negative or positive feedback, people with social phobia will concentrate on detecting specifically negative feedback. As a result, they will be much better than others at detecting any real negative feedback but will be much worse at detecting positive feedback. In addition, they will often tend to distort the information they receive so that neutral information will frequently be interpreted as negative. As a result, external feedback to the mental representation of appearance will be strongly negatively biased.

Finally, people with social phobia will also develop an anticipation of the performance standard that an audience will expect from them. They frequently assume that any given audience will hold a higher expectation for their performance than will people without social phobia. In addition, the expected standard will rise or fall depending on the situation. For example, they may believe that attractive people expect better performance than do unattractive people or that members of the opposite sex hold higher standards than do members of the same sex.

The next step in the model is the combination of these pieces of information. The mental representation of how the individual is coming across to others is compared with the standard that the individual believes these others expect. If the appearance or performance falls short of the assumed standard, this will, in turn, produce an increase in the degree to which the audience is likely to evaluate the individual negatively. The consequences of this negative evaluation are also likely to be inflated in people with social phobia. The degree and consequences of expected negative evaluation will directly determine the degree of anxiety/embarrassment.

Important to the maintenance of the overall anxiety in the situation is feedback from the consequences of the anxiety. Anxiety is manifested in a combination of increased physiological arousal, increased negative thoughts, and withdrawal/avoidance behaviors. According to the model, when an individual becomes anxious in a situation, these features will feed back to the person's mental representation of how she appears to others, further distorting it and hence further maintaining or even increasing the anxiety. One of the more important sources of feedback also comes via the individual's behaviors. People with social phobia frequently engage in subtle avoidance behaviors. For example, a person may avert her gaze while speaking to people in the hope of being overlooked. Or she may stand on the periphery of a group with a hunched and closed posture so as not to be an object of attention. In these cases the person may appear to lack basic social skills, but it is not so much a lack of knowledge of the skills but a lack of use of skills as a consequence of anxiety. In turn, this subtle avoidance behavior will reduce engagement with the audience, providing further negative feedback to the individual.

TREATMENT RATIONALE

The treatment program described in this book is based on a large body of empirical evidence. Components of the treatment are aimed at altering various stages of the maintenance model described above.

The treatment program involves several components. We begin with provision of basic information about social phobia to provide a framework for the client to better understand the nature of her disorder and its treatment. We next introduce cognitive restructuring strategies aimed at helping the client to alter her fundamental exaggerated beliefs. In terms of the model, it is important to alter several types of beliefs: (1) that others will appraise her negatively, (2) that she is actually incompetent, (3) that others hold high expectations for her performance, and (4) that if others think negatively of her, that is a tragedy.

The third component of the treatment package is one specifically predicted by the model. We teach clients to refocus their attention away from their mental representation of how they appear to others and away from negative feedback from others and toward the task at hand. This will help to improve performance and, in turn, will result in more positive feedback from others.

Fourth, clients are taught exposure exercises in order to learn through direct experience that negative evaluation is not likely and that even if it occurs, it is not the end of the world. It is important to address subtle avoidance and to ensure that clients expose themselves to all aspects of a situation that pose potential threat.

Finally, the issue of social performance is addressed in an attempt to directly alter exaggerated aspects of the client's mental representation of how she appears to others. This component involves a combination of feedback about social performance and teaching or practicing of social skills where necessary.

As mentioned earlier, treatment packages such as this one have been extensively tested in an empirical fashion. Results have been strong, indicating that the majority of participants receive at least some benefit (Heimberg and Juster 1995). Outcome has been shown to be superior to waitlist as well as to placebo treatment. For example, Heimberg and colleagues (1990) compared a cognitive behavioral treatment (CBT) package conducted in a group format with a placebo treatment composed of education and group support. Importantly, both treatments were rated equally credible by participants. The results indicated that the CBT package was somewhat superior to the education group at post-treatment and especially so at six-month follow-up. More recently, Richard Heimberg, Michael Liebowitz and colleagues (1997) repeated this comparison and added two other groups that received either phenelzine or a pill placebo. Short-term results indicated that both cognitive behavioral treatment and phenelzine were effective in reducing social phobia and were significantly better than either placebo condition. Phenelzine had a more rapid effect. However, in the longer term, people who stopped taking phenelzine often relapsed, whereas those in the cognitive-behavioral treatment maintained their gains (Liebowitz, Heimberg et al. 1997). A list of empirical studies that have tested these types of treatment packages is provided in Suggested Further Readings on p. 159.

In the following chapters we will provide explicit detail about the delivery of the treatment package to people with social phobia. Sample monitoring forms are provided and, where possible, potential difficulties are preempted. In Chapter 3 we describe a typical case of social phobia and use this case throughout the book to illustrate treatment application. A further advantage is the provision of a client manual that goes with this package (*Overcoming Shyness and Social Phobia*, Rapee 1998). This book has been written directly for the lay public and follows the current treatment package in a parallel format. It also contains sample monitoring forms, suggested exercises, and extensive case illustrations. It is important to point out that the client book was written as an adjunct to the current treatment, not as a replacement. Ideally, clients would receive a copy of the client manual to help reinforce the sessions with the therapist and aid homework practice.

The various components of the treatment program are described in separate chapters. However, it is worth repeating that the program does not need to be conducted by allocating one session per chapter. Individual clients will work at different rates and will all have their own complexities. Ideally, you should stay with a particular treatment component for as long as it takes your client to master the principles. You can also return to some components when difficulties arise. Nevertheless, some therapists will be working under the constraints of a restricted treatment duration, such as managed care. In these instances, working through one component of this package per session will provide a comprehensive, eight-session treatment program for social phobia. In such cases, the client manual will be especially valuable. A sample outline for such a program is given in Table 2–1.

A WORD ABOUT GROUPS

We have described the treatment package in this book from the perspective of individual treatment. This is the format of choice for most practicing professionals because the practicalities of referral rates and timetabling make group formats difficult. Nevertheless, the current treatment package lends itself ideally to delivery in a group format. Few adjustments will need to be made and exactly the same principles and procedures can be followed. In fact, given that the central fears in social phobia relate to other people, group treatment of people with social phobia has many advantages over individual treatment. It provides automatic exposure, allows for regular peer feedback, and provides a perfect forum for role play and skills practice. If you are able to organize group treatment for social phobia, you will find that most clients will have little difficulty with this

Table 2–1. Outline of eight-session treatment program.

Pre-treatment	Diagnostic interview and assessment
Session 1	1. Building rapport. 2. Providing information about social phobia. 3. Providing a treatment rationale. 4. Instigating self monitoring.
Session 2	1. Providing rationale for cognitive restructuring. 2. Commencing monitoring and identifying beliefs. 3. Challenging the probability of negative outcomes.
Session 3	1. Challenging the consequences of negative outcomes. 2. Practicing and applying cognitive restruc turing.
Session 4	1. Providing a rationale for attention training. 2. Teaching attention-strengthening exercises. 3. Applying attention strengthening in vivo.
Session 5	1. Providing a rationale for in vivo exposure 2. Developing an exposure hierarchy. 3. Setting a timetable and goals for in vivo exposure exercises.
Session 6	1. Assessing real or perceived limits in social performance. 2. Learning to obtain feedback about social performance. 3. Teaching and practicing social skills.
Session 7	1. Discussing practice and application of techniques to the real world. 2. Applying techniques to special individual problems.
Session 8	1. Discussing practice and application. 2. Reviewing program, techniques, and progress. 3. Discussing future practice and goals. 4. Raising the possibility of relapse and its prevention.

concept and many will actually welcome it. For those who are a little reticent, encouragement will usually get them there and they will almost always relax after the first or second session. You may come across the occasional highly avoidant person who will not be willing to enter a group format. In this case, it may be a good idea to provide a few individual sessions first to work on decreasing the client's fear of entering the group.

3

A Case of Social Phobia

John B. is a 32-year-old single male who contacted us for treatment because, as he described it, "I finally need to do something to become more confident." John reported that his life is completely restricted due to his fears of other people. When questioned in more detail about specific feared situations, John reported that he becomes anxious in a broad variety of places and activities involving others. Some of his most problematic situations include working in front of other colleagues; doing the shopping at his local mall; meeting any new person, especially women; and having to make inquiries on the phone. Whenever possible, John would avoid these activities and any others where people were present such as going out to exhibitions, eating at restaurants, or shopping for new clothes. When asked about the type of thoughts or beliefs that go through John's mind when he has to do any of these activities, he said that he feels as if everyone is watching him and that they are judging him negatively. For example, John believes that he has an unusual walk and that people stare at him behind his back and laugh about how odd he looks. He also has a number of other negative beliefs, specifically, that he is not very attractive and not very smart. When John does interact with other people, especially particularly frightening ones such as females or people of high status, he says that he usually breaks out in a sweat, begins to shake, and his mind goes completely blank so that he loses his train of thought.

John has few friends and believes that other people are unlikely to want to get to know someone as uninteresting as he is. He has two friends—one from work with whom he goes out occasionally and the other, a neighbor, with whom he sometimes goes to ball games. Aside from this, John spends most of his time alone, usually at home watching TV or doing crossword puzzles. He says that he enjoys his own company but would certainly like to meet a few more friends.

John has never had a serious romantic relationship. He has been on only a few dates in his life—mainly arranged through his father when he was in high school—and has only had sexual experiences with prostitutes. This is a source of central concern to John who says that at 32, he feels time is running out to meet a partner and raise a family. He reports being terrified whenever he talks to women and says that he never knows what to say.

John is employed as a postal worker, occasionally delivering mail, but more often working in the sorting room and office. He works hard and is well thought of by his boss. Recently, John was offered a chance for a higher-level position but refused it because it would involve organizing other people and working to some extent with the public. John says that he often asks for night shifts because there are fewer people around and he can work more easily by himself. He says that he likes his job because it is nonthreatening but worries that eventually he will have to move on.

John was raised as the only child of parents who were somewhat older when they had him. His mother was 38 and his father 51. John's mother died of cancer when he was only 10 and he was raised during his teens by his father. John describes his father as a stern man who did not show a great deal of affection and did not tend to socialize very much. They would socialize occasionally with relatives in the next state, but John did not describe himself as close to these family members.

John recalled that he has always been a shy person. For as far back as he can remember he describes himself as a relative loner. He always had one or two good friends in school, but they were generally quiet, like himself, and he was never a central figure in his classes. He spent much of his school life trying to avoid being the center of attention, not asking questions in class and never joining team sports. John says that his main memories of childhood are ones that would be summarized as "happy but quiet."

Aside from his problems with other people, John says that lately he has begun to feel a little down. He went through a week a few months ago when he felt very teary, lost interest in most activities, had decreased appetite, and had trouble sleeping. Aside from this, John does not report any other major problems with depression, but says that in recent months he has begun to be plagued by thoughts that he will never have a family and his life will never amount to anything. In addition to these negative thoughts, John reports that over the past year or so, he has begun to find solace in drinking. He says that he has a few beers when he gets home from work on most days in order "to unwind." In addition, he says that recently he has discovered that interacting with other people is easier if he has a drink or two before going out. Occasionally, he has even had a drink before going to work in order to help him through the shift.

Based on information at interview, John appears to meet diagnostic criteria for Social Phobia (generalized type). It was not believed that his dysthymic symptoms and substance abuse were of sufficient severity to warrant diagnoses, but note was made to keep a close eye on these features. In addition, John technically meets criteria for an Axis II diagnosis of Avoidant Personality Disorder. However, his desire to learn to interact with others and develop a romantic relationship suggests that this may not be a major negative prognostic indicator, because John is still likely to be motivated to overcome his social fears.

COMMENTS

John's case illustrates a fairly typical picture of severe social phobia. The severity of his case, exemplified by his extensive life restrictions and lack of social support, is prognostically negative and indicates that he will not be easy to treat. In addition, the mild depressed mood and alcohol abuse may provide difficulties in terms of motivation and attitude change. On the other hand, John appears motivated and has clear reasons for wanting to improve. He also reports a number of clearly definable behaviors that can form the central focus for treatment intervention.

Throughout the remainder of this book, we will use John's case to illustrate the application of the various treatment components.

Treatment of
Social Phobia

4

Information and
Self-Monitoring

AIMS

1. Getting to know your client.
2. Establishing rapport and helping your client feel comfortable with you.
3. Giving your client an understanding of social phobia.
4. Explaining the treatment rationale.
5. Beginning self-monitoring.

Building Rapport and Getting to Know Your Client

All good therapies, empirically based or otherwise, share a number of common, central features. There is ample evidence that all treatments and techniques are more effective when presented by a warm, empathic therapist. It is a common misconception that empirically based, manualized therapies can be presented in a formula-driven, mechanistic fashion. Nothing could be further from the truth. The therapist–client relationship is just as important to empirically based therapies as it is to any other form of treatment. This may be even more so with social phobia than many other disorders. People with social phobia worry about what others think of them. As an important, high-status other, you will feature prominently in your client's concerns, especially at your first meeting. Therefore, much of the first session should be spent breaking the ice and helping your client to feel more comfortable with you and to build enthusiasm and hope for the treatment program.

If you have previously interviewed your client in order to arrive at a diagnosis, much of the material covered in this section will already have been done. However, if you were not the one to conduct the diagnosis, or if this is your first session, then it is naturally very important to obtain information about the symptoms, thoughts, and feelings of the client. This serves the dual purpose of providing you with necessary information and providing both of you with a common task during which the relationship can develop. You need to be thoroughly familiar with Chapter 1, in which the assessment and diagnosis of social phobia is discussed. Make sure you obtain a thorough understanding of the idiosyncratic ways in which your client manifests her fears and behaviors. In particular, you need to question your client closely about the parameters that affect her fears such as status, gender, occupation, and so on. In addition, you need to get a good understanding of subtle forms of avoidance such as avoiding eye contact, always going to functions with a significant other, wearing certain clothing, and so on. Finally, developing an understanding of the underlying beliefs that your client holds in various situations will be very useful in appreciating her motivations (e.g., "I am generally incompetent," "I look ugly," "Others tend to be very critical," etc.). Whereas much of this information can and will be obtained and elaborated as you proceed through therapy, questioning these issues at this point serves two purposes. First, it helps you to gain a better overall understanding of your client which, in turn, will help to fine-tune the treatment program. Second, it helps to strengthen rapport and your credibility. Asking highly relevant questions will help reinforce to your client that you are experienced in dealing with her problem, that you understand its nature, and that she is not alone in her concerns.

Explaining Social Phobia

Once you have spent sufficient time discussing the client's problem, it is very important to provide a general description of social phobia and an understanding of possible causal and maintaining factors. Most clients have a lot of questions such as, "Are there others like me?," and "Why am I like this?" Providing answers to these questions is a vital part of treatment because it helps to give the client a sense of hope for improvement and also improves trust in your expertise. More important, by providing an understanding of the maintaining factors in the problem, you are in a position to help the client understand the purpose and rationale behind the treatment. In turn, this will help both the application and motivation for the treatment.

Information about the nature and maintenance of social phobia can basically follow the material provided in Chapter 2. Naturally, you will need to present the information in terms the client can understand and you will need to adjust both the content and language to your client's educational level. Clients also differ in their needs. Some don't care about facts and figures; others want to know all about them. At the very least, clients do need to develop an appreciation of maintaining factors in their problem in order to understand the treatment rationale. A good basic coverage of the relevant information, presented in lay terms, is provided in the client guide (Rapee 1998). Naturally, it is often a good idea to make the presentation of information as personal as possible. At each point you may want to ask the client to identify similarities in her own case. For example, when talking about the fact that social phobia runs in families, the client might be able to identify other family members who are shy. Similarly, when discussing the central role of fear of negative evaluation, you may ask your client to identify some of her own thoughts that relate to this concept.

Some of the specific points that we try to make to most clients are given below. We have written most of this in the language we would use with clients, although you will probably need to expand on many aspects in your own way.

1. Social phobia is really the same sort of thing as shyness. Therefore you (the client) are not crazy and you don't have some sort of disease or illness. Rather, we are talking about your characteristic way of relating and reacting to the world which, at times, interferes with other aspects of your life.

2. This state is normal. We all feel shy at certain times and in certain situations. Furthermore, it is beneficial. People who never feel shy are often socially inappropriate and are not the sort of people many of us want to be around. Social concerns help us to fit in with society and to do the right or socially accepted thing in numerous circumstances. Some people are simply more shy than others. The difference between you and people who do not come in for help is simply that you have realized that your shyness is holding you back or in some way interfering with your life.

3. Why some people are more shy than others is not completely known. However, it almost certainly has a lot to do with our genes. We know that there is probably no direct "shyness" gene. Rather, what people inherit probably has more to do with the general degree to which they are emotional. You are probably a fairly emotional person in general. Because a lot of this is genetic, there is a limit to how much we can change. But it is important to point out that we wouldn't necessarily want to change it, even if we could. Your emotionality has both good and bad aspects. On the negative side, you are shy. You might also be anxious in other ways and even suffer depression. However, on the positive side, you are probably sensitive, caring,

and honest. If we were able to change the entire you, your partner/friends/family would probably stop liking you. So, all we want to do is to help you to control the extremes in your shyness so that they no longer interfere with your life. We certainly wouldn't want to change the entire you, even if we could.

4. Your shyness has probably also come from a number of other factors in your life. These might include things you learned from your parents, ways your parents raised you, and specific events that have happened to you. The main point is that these things are over. We don't know exactly what caused your shyness and we can't change them. What we need to do is help you change your way of relating to the world here and now so that you learn to overcome your shyness. This is certainly possible.

5. There are several things that researchers have identified that help to keep you socially anxious. First, there is your thinking style. People with social phobia are very concerned with what we call *negative evaluation*—that is, with the possibility that other people will think badly of them. Certainly, there are some times when someone may well think badly of you. But this is usually not that common. The main point is that people with social phobia tend to believe that others will think badly of them far more than is realistic. In addition, people with social phobia tend to believe that others thinking badly of them is far worse than is realistic. In other words, people with social phobia often believe that, if others think badly of them, this is an *absolute tragedy*. People who are not shy don't think this way. Therefore, one thing we need to do in treatment is to teach you that other people are not always going to think badly of you and even if they do, it is probably not an absolute tragedy. It is unrealistic to be liked by everyone and most people's opinions will have no direct impact on your life.

   Another thing you probably do that helps to maintain your problem is paying too much attention to the wrong things. There is evidence that when people with social phobia are performing in a situation, a large part of their attention is paid to imagining what other people are thinking about them and also how they look and sound to those other people. If this is the case, then they are not paying full attention to what they are doing or to what they are saying. So, another part of our treatment program will involve teaching you to pay more attention where you need to and less to unnecessary things.

Finally, your problem is being maintained largely because you avoid those things you are frightened of doing. By avoiding things, you convince yourself that they really are difficult and that you really can't do them. So a large part of our program will involve getting you to do the things you are currently not doing in order to prove to yourself that you can do them. (Note to the therapist: some clients who do not avoid in obvious ways may argue that avoidance is not an issue in their case. It is very important that you explain that avoidance can involve subtle forms as well as obvious ones.)

Treatment Rationale

Following the discussion of the maintaining factors in social phobia, the treatment rationale should now make a great deal of sense to the client. You will probably have already discussed many aspects of it and there is certainly no need to keep it as a separate component. However, it never hurts to have regular repetition for clients who are often psychologically unsophisticated. In addition, it is probably a good idea to summarize the maintaining factors in the context of explaining how treatment will proceed. To this end, the use of a summary list may be a valuable aid.

We have included a possible summary below (see Table 4–1). You can use it to briefly cover the primary maintaining factors and then to explain how each factor will be addressed with a specific component of treatment. Naturally, you would want to describe the treat-

Table 4–1. Summary of treatment rationale.

Maintaining Factors	Treatment Technique
Excessive thoughts about negative evaluation	Education and training in realistic thinking
Focusing of attention onto negatives and away from the task at hand	Training in attention strengthening and increasing awareness of correct focus
Avoidance of social situations and subtle avoidance of involvement in social events	Gradual exposure to feared situations and feedback and training in social skills

ment components in more detail than you had previously. When describing exposure, it is very important that you first explain to your client that she will have learned coping strategies by that stage and thus she will be better able to deal with the situation. In addition, exposure is done gradually and the pace is entirely under her control. Without explaining these points, you may find your client not turning up next week! Naturally, you will need to allow plenty of time for her to ask questions and you should determine how logical and helpful the treatment sounds to her.

Self-Monitoring

Self-monitoring of various behaviors, thoughts, and events is an extremely valuable component of treatment. It provides valuable information for you about your client's life and can help you to tailor treatment to her specific needs. More important, self-monitoring helps to increase awareness and insight for the client. Most people are very poor observers of their own behavior, so engaging in a few weeks of recording can really open up a rich tapestry of detail.

There are several things that can be monitored at this early stage of treatment. We describe one monitoring form (Table 4–2) that is broadly useful. (This form is also included in the Client Manual.) On this form, the client records the situations that she feared or

Table 4–2. Form to be used for monitoring of features of social phobia.

Social Situations Record

Degree of nervousness or shyness

0	1	2	3	4	5	6	7	8

none　　　　slight　　　　moderate　　　　quite a bit　　　　extreme

Situation or Event	Negative Thoughts	Anxiety/Shyness (0–8)	Physical Symptoms	Avoidance or Other Behaviors

avoided that day as well as her beliefs, degree of anxiety, and reactions to each situation. Proper use of this form can help to identify such information as the breadth of situations feared and their interference in life; the underlying cognitions; and the variety of emotional, physical, and behavioral reactions to these situations. However, depending on idiosyncratic aspects of your client, you may decide that other things are more important for her to monitor. If so, it is easy to design your own monitoring form and substitute one or more aspects.

There is a very important point to be made about self-monitoring. Monitoring is generally an effortful and unpleasant task to perform and clients will not do it unless they believe it is of value. The therapist must spend time pointing out the value of self-monitoring, empathizing with the intrusiveness, and highlighting the importance of doing it correctly. In addition, the client will only monitor week by week to the extent that you treat it as important. That is, if you spend time each week going over the prior week's monitoring, it will generally get done. But if you begin to ignore it, so will the client. Finally, clients will often forget about their monitoring at first and will sometimes complete their forms just before the next treatment session so that the therapist is not annoyed with them. This is especially so for social phobics. It is probably a good idea at the next session to inquire about how the monitoring went, how difficult it was, and when it was done. It is also very important to normalize the difficulty and resistance toward doing homework assignments in order to facilitate discussion, especially among social phobic clients who may be less likely to admit to not doing homework. Then you can repeat your discussion about how important it is and urge the client to really try to put effort into this task.

Homework

There are two main parts to homework in this component.

First, the client should read the section in the client manual (or something equivalent that you may have produced) on the nature and maintaining factors of social phobia and the treatment rationale. The more understanding and insight the client develops, the better. This will help to provide the client with realistic treatment expectations and will stress the importance of being active in treatment. Second, the client should monitor her thoughts, feelings, and behaviors in feared situations (or in anticipation of feared situations, including those that were avoided). This should be continued for at least two weeks to get a good sample of these situations. It will also reinforce to the client the impact that the problem is having on her life.

Dealing with Difficulties

In most cases, people with social phobia will be quite willing to open up and confide all of their concerns to a therapist. Given the prior expectations of coming to a therapeutic situation, this will be no different for the social phobic than for anyone else. However, in some severe cases, especially where avoidant personality features are prominent, there will be a degree of suspicion and a natural tendency not to reveal intimate aspects of the self. In these cases it is best to proceed, for the present, at an easy pace. Let the client know that she should feel free to tell you if she does not wish to discuss certain issues. Perhaps you might also limit your questions at this stage to relatively superficial topics such as symptoms and feared situations and avoid intimate ones, such as sexual or relationship issues. It is very important not to appear at all confrontational. If, for example, you pick up on inconsistencies in the story, it is best to make a note of these for later reference rather than pointing them out at the moment. A person who lacks trust is at high risk not to return to the next session if she senses any threat from you. Over the coming weeks, as the relationship develops and the client invests more in you, you can gently raise confusing or intimate issues. In a sense, you are providing for these clients a form of exposure and also a demonstration that they can confide in others without being hurt.

By moving at a pace that is too rapid for the client's comfort level, you risk losing her altogether. These issues are discussed in more detail in Chapter 10.

Another difficult client is the one who is vague, unstructured, and focuses on general malaise rather than on specific issues. She may also jump easily from problem to problem. Many of these clients have been previously treated in traditional analytical therapies and have become used to a free-floating, unstructured therapeutic style. It is very important to be highly structured with such clients from the outset, probably more so than you would be with most others. You need to operationalize concepts for them repeatedly and keep them on track. If the client wanders from problem to problem, one effective strategy is to redirect her to the initial problem and discuss the advantage of staying with that problem before moving on to a new one. To ensure that the client is focusing on relevant issues, one useful tack is to ask her to describe exactly how that problem interferes with her life and in what precise ways it is a problem. Clearly, you need to listen to, empathize with, and understand the client's feelings. But following this general empathy, it is important to direct the therapy. Focusing on clear behaviors is the best way to help these clients achieve practical gains.

5

~

Cognitive Restructuring—I

AIMS

1. Discussing homework.
2. Gaining knowledge of the rationale and mechanisms of cognitive restructuring.
3. Beginning cognitive restructuring and developing insight regarding unrealistic beliefs.
4. Reassessing excessive probabilities.

COGNITIVE RESTRUCTURING: OVERVIEW

There is considerable empirical evidence to indicate that anxious individuals tend to overestimate the probability and cost of threatening events. In a recent study, Edna Foa and colleagues (1996) demonstrated that social phobics rated both the probability and cost of negative social events (e.g., someone you know won't say hello to you) as higher than did nonclinical subjects. This effect was not found on negative nonsocial events. In addition, the change in the estimated cost of negative social events was the best predictor of treatment outcome. The main purpose of cognitive restructuring then, is to teach clients to view events from a more realistic perspective.

There is a variety of forms of cognitive restructuring and most are based on very similar principles. The form that we favor is primarily based on the pioneering work of Aaron Beck (Beck, Emery, and Greenberg 1985). This is an evidence-based technique in which clients are taught to first identify their irrational beliefs and then to examine factual evidence to determine how rational and/or accurate the belief is. For many problems, the therapist's role, via a series of questions and observations, is to help the client to view situations in a more realistic fashion. However, the current program also works on the principle that clients should be taught the general rules of the various techniques so that they can administer therapy to themselves across various situations. In this way, clients ultimately learn to be independent of the therapist. Therefore, in this program we will be going through a highly stylized form of cognitive restructuring that is taught to the client as a set of rules and procedures that can be applied across situations. The therapist teaches the basic techniques and then, week by week, goes through numerous examples from the preceding week. This procedure allows each of these specific situations to be dealt with, but more important, the focus is on encouraging the client to gradually do more and more of the work in order to become more skilled at changing his own thinking style.

There is also likely to be a number of major and difficult scenarios that you as the therapist may need to work through together with the client. At times, when these scenarios are particularly complex, working through one may take an entire session. For example, you may feel the need to work through certain attitudes your client has about his parents or childhood. More commonly with social phobics, there may be certain basic "life scripts" that require detailed discussion such as the need to always be popular or to always do a perfect job. If such issues are important, it is best to teach the basic principles of cognitive restructuring first in the context of numerous everyday examples. Then, when the client appears to be more comfortable with the basic concepts of cognitive restructuring, you may want to spend a session or two specifically covering these difficult and more fundamental issues.

RATIONALE FOR COGNITIVE RESTRUCTURING

There is considerable empirical evidence to indicate that anxious individuals tend to overestimate the probability of threatening events. One of the first studies in this area was conducted by Gilian Butler and Andrew Mathews (1983). In their study, they asked people with generalized anxiety disorder and nonclinical subjects to report the probability that negative events would happen to them or to someone else. They found that the anxious subjects reported significantly higher probabilities for negative events happening to themselves. Similar findings have since been determined for socially phobic individuals and, in this case, the effect is only found for negative social events (Foa et al. 1996).

As with all new procedures, it is very important that the client receive a good rationale for how and why the technique should work. We generally begin with an everyday example. The example should provide a common scenario in which a person is likely to experience changing emotions based only on differing information he might have at various times. Importantly, the actual facts of the situation should not change. For example "Imagine that your partner is late getting home. How would you feel?" The client will probably answer "worried" or "angry." "Then imagine that you suddenly remember that your partner told you that s/he was going out tonight and would be getting home late. Now how would you feel?" We hope the client will answer "relaxed." The important issue is that the fact of the situation—that the partner is late arriving home—has not changed. All that has changed is the information the client has and, hence, the beliefs or thoughts inside his head, or the way the client has *appraised* the situation.

The fundamental rule that clients need to be taught is: *External facts, events, and situations do not* directly *lead to emotions. Rather, emotions come* directly *from our beliefs, attitudes, and thoughts. External events only result in emotions after being perceived or interpreted in some way.* Typically, for an emotion to be generated, the situation must be appraised as having some personal meaning to the individual (e.g., "If that person doesn't smile at me, it means he doesn't like the way I look"). Pathological negative emotions result from systematic misappraisals. (Social phobic clients consistently appraise negative evaluation from others.) This fundamental rule of cognitive restructuring will need to be repeated to clients over and over. Following from the preceding rule is its corollary: *If we can learn to control our beliefs, attitudes, and interpretations, at least to some extent, then to that extent, we can control our emotions* (*especially those that result from cognitive distortions*).

At this point, most clients will have several burning questions or even disagreements. You can stop here and address any questions or discuss any concerns. Alternately, you may find it more convincing to preempt some of the most likely questions (some of these may not even be thought of until clients go home) and address these before they are raised. There are three main issues that we usually discuss.

Some clients are concerned that they are going to be made into computers, always controlling their emotions. Even worse, some clients are excited by this prospect since the prospect of always being in control of one's emotions feeds nicely into their social concerns. Clients need to be clearly informed that the point of the technique is not to try to control all emotions. Further, this would not be possible, even if they wanted to. Many beliefs and attitudes are too entrenched and, in fact, logical, to be changed. Therefore, even if your client becomes really good at cognitive restructuring, he will still be basically the same person and will still "feel" in much the same way. Instead, the purpose of cognitive restructuring is to be able to change those emotions that are excessive or too extreme. Just as it is our beliefs that directly lead to our emotions, it is excessive beliefs that lead to excessive emotions. What we aim to do through cognitive restructuring is to tone down these extreme beliefs.

The second issue some clients will raise is that they do not think when they get into a difficult situation; rather, their embarrassment or anxiety just seems to hit them without warning. Cognitive psychologists have known for years that much of our behavior is determined by processes that are below conscious awareness. In his descriptions of cognitive restructuring, Aaron Beck describes what he calls "automatic thoughts." This is precisely why we prefer to talk about "attitudes" or "beliefs," because they sound less conscious and carefully thought out than "thoughts." Clients need to be informed that their thoughts or attitudes are not always (and in fact are rarely) thought out in a deliberate, conscious manner. For example, if someone points a gun at us, we don't sit there for a few seconds while we think to ourselves, "Gee, I think I'm going to get killed, now." Rather, our appraisal occurs very rapidly and automatically, so that we are often not even aware of it. It only *appears* as though we just react. Nevertheless, our reaction is still mediated by our beliefs. If we were from Mars and did not know what a gun was, we would not be frightened because we would not have the understanding that guns are dangerous and hence we would not fear for our lives.

Some clients will raise the concern at this point that if our beliefs are automatic then we can never change them. You may then need to discuss the fact that automatic processes can be changed. It is just much slower and harder to do than to change more obvious, conscious processes. Changing automatic processes requires a lot of rehearsal. You might give an example such as seeing a red light when driving. We are all trained to step on the brake when we see a red light. This is generally an automatic process—we certainly don't have to give it much conscious thought before we respond. If the government were to enact a law that swapped red and green lights so we now had to stop at green lights, we would all find this very hard to do. However, we could do it. First we would need to make our actions conscious, that is consciously think to ourselves when we see a green light, "I need to step on the brake now." But, over time and with lots and lots of practice, we would eventually push the brake in response to the green light without even realizing it. It is precisely the same principle that holds in relation to our beliefs.

The third issue we usually bring up is an interesting one. Over the years, several of our clients have smiled knowingly as we discussed cognitive restructuring and have nodded enthusiastically at various points. Then, when we finished our spiel, they have said, "Ah, yes, I already do this. I practice my positive affirmations every day." Stemming originally from Norman Vincent Peale's *The Power of Positive Thinking*, much of the lay world has picked up on the notion that to overcome problems, we simply need to think happy thoughts. As a result, many people confuse cognitive restructuring with so-called "positive thinking." Of course, these are very different, but for the later teaching of cognitive restructuring, it is vitally important that your client understand how and why they are different. Otherwise, you will find yourself with several problems down the road.

The fundamental difference between positive thinking and cognitive restructuring is in the power of belief. In order for cognitive restructuring to have an effect, the client must believe what he is saying to himself. Positive thinking often fails to work because it is very difficult for people to completely believe it. In fact, positive thinking is a distortion in the opposite direction from what they are used to. An example we often use for clients is to think about what happens if someone close to them dies. Positive thinking would say, "Don't be sad, it's probably for the best." Of course, in most circumstances, it is very hard to believe that this is so. When discussing cognitive restructuring with clients, we generally use the term *realistic thinking*. This term provides the information to the client that the basic principle is to think realistically about his situation. Our thinking is often unrealistic, and in these cases, thinking more realistically should help to change our emotions. However, there are times, such as the example above, when it is quite realistic and perfectly all right to feel a certain emotion, such as sadness. Basically, life sometimes sucks, and it is quite OK to feel angry, hurt, sad, or scared under certain circumstances. Simply telling oneself that a situation is not bad will not change one's feelings. You have to *believe* what you are saying to yourself for it to have any effect. For cognitive restructuring to work, the new thoughts must be more realistic than the old ones in order to supersede them. When clients allow themselves to be human and feel a variety of emotions, they are more likely to believe alternate information at times when it is logical to do so.

Step 1: *Identifying Cognitions and Unrealistic Beliefs*

As we discussed earlier, many manifestations of beliefs that arise in a threatening situation are automatic and not obviously available to consciousness. Therefore, the first, and probably most important step in cognitive restructuring is for the client to learn to identify his beliefs in social situations.

Quite simply, the client needs to practice asking himself certain questions each time he begins to feel anxious. Each client will respond best to a particular question. The purpose is for the client to understand the concept, not to learn a rote question. Some sample questions might be: "Why am I feeling anxious here?" "What terrible thing am I expecting here?" "What could happen to me that is so bad?" "What am I thinking right now?", and so forth. The main idea is for the client to determine the most pressing negative prediction for the situation. Some common thoughts/beliefs reported by people with social phobia are as follows.

- They must think I look really silly.
- I am going to blow this.
- I look ridiculous.

- They are going to laugh at me.
- They will realize how incompetent I am.
- They won't think very much of me.
- Everyone here is better at this than I am.
- I won't know what to say.

There are some "rules" in reporting the initial belief that can help to make the procedure much smoother. The initial belief should always be phrased as a direct, unequivocal statement. That is, it should be a prediction of what dire consequence the individual expects will happen. Often a client will try to report his belief in terms of a question; such as, "I wonder if they will like me?" By phrasing it as a question, the client seems to imply that he is *unsure* whether the people will or will not like him. If this were truly his belief, he would probably not be very anxious. Typically, anxiety is mediated not by such a mix of positive and negative, but by expecting the negative side of the equation. In other words, if the client is feeling anxious, it is because he believes that there is a strong likelihood that people in the situation will not like him. Therefore, in order to work with the anxious part of the belief, this negative part should be phrased in the form of a straightforward statement, in this case, "They will not like me."

Clients should be taught to distinguish between thoughts and emotions and not to include emotions in their initial presentation of beliefs. An initial belief statement such as "I will feel anxious" is best avoided because it is merely descriptive of the expected emotion and is not getting at the underlying cognitive factors mediating the anxiety. While it is not impossible, it is often very difficult to work with emotions as the feared event. This is largely because the whole exercise becomes rather circular. After all, our whole premise is that many emotions are not inevitable, but may or may not occur, depending upon one's evaluation of a situation. Therefore, the way to alleviate anxiety is to apply cognitive restructuring to the evaluation of the situation. In other words, it is very difficult to determine evidence for the belief "I will feel anxious," because it depends on how well one performs cognitive restructuring. If cognitive restructuring is not successful, then it is probably an accurate belief to say that one will become anxious in a social situation. However, this is simply a reflection of the negative thinking pattern.

When clients come up with initial beliefs that center around an emotion, they should be encouraged to ask an additional question of themselves such as, "What am I expecting in this situation that is going to make me feel anxious?" An example from a therapy session follows.

THERAPIST: Tell me about a situation that is generally difficult for you.

CLIENT: Well, one of the worst things is I have to go and meet with my boss.

THERAPIST: OK, let's try to imagine that you are about to do that. Tell me, what's the first thought that comes to mind?

CLIENT: That's easy—I'm going to panic.

THERAPIST: That's an understandable thought, but remember what we spoke about earlier. An emotion such as panic will not inevitably happen. It depends entirely on how well we do this exercise together. What we need to find out is *why* do you think you're going to panic? What do you expect in your meeting that will make you panic?

CLIENT: I guess it's that I expect that my boss will hate my work.

THERAPIST: So an initial belief we can work with is that "the boss will hate my work."

An additional point needs to be made here. It is true that clients should be steered away from centering their initial belief on an overall emotion. However, the somatic component of such emotions do not suffer the same limitations. Therefore, an initial belief along the lines

"I will blush" or "I will shake" is quite acceptable and is often a very good one to work with.

Finally, clients need to be told to be honest in the beliefs they identify. Quite often the initial belief, and even more often the underlying beliefs (to be discussed later), will seem quite illogical and ridiculous when one verbalizes them. But these are precisely the thoughts one needs to move from unconscious to conscious. You should remind your client about the importance of honesty and openness in therapy, about the fact that keeping things hidden is only hurting him, and the fact that only you, the therapist, and he will see any of what is written. In fact, if your client has a problem with your seeing some of his thoughts, you might even suggest that he edit what he shows you. (Later, editing can be reduced.) It is very important that you explain to your client that if thoughts are left unexamined and below awareness, they can never be evaluated and ultimately changed. Our extreme emotions are often mediated by seemingly very "crazy" beliefs, and this is precisely why we need to make them explicit—so that we can change them. As a rule, it is a good idea to suggest to your client that if a thought enters his mind, no matter what he thinks of it, he should write it down because the fact that it is there indicates that it is probably having an impact on his emotions.

Step 2: Evaluating Evidence

When an individual states a belief regarding an expected outcome in a situation, it is generally connected to the implication that this outcome is definitely going to occur. Clearly, this will produce maximum anxiety. For example, believing "they will definitely laugh at me" is enough to make anyone anxious. Obviously, then, the lower the expected probability that the negative event will occur, the lower the anxiety. A belief that "there is a 20 percent chance that they will laugh at me" should produce far less anxiety than the belief that "they will definitely laugh at me." The purpose of the cognitive restructuring procedure is to help clients to lower the probability with which they expect negative events to occur. However, as discussed earlier, the effectiveness of the procedure is based on *belief*. Simply getting a client to say to himself, "I'm sure it won't happen" will not accomplish anything if he doesn't believe it. Therefore, the final decision regarding the probability of the negative outcome must be realistic in the client's mind.

To this end, we teach clients to evaluate the evidence for the initial belief, helping them come to a more factual conclusion and thus be more likely to believe the newly derived probability. The question clients need to ask here is "How do I know that such and such will occur?" or "What evidence do I have as to whether such and such will or will not occur?" The way we often describe this process to clients is that they have to become scientists with respect to their own behavior. Instead of beliefs being seen as factual statements, they should be treated as hypotheses that need to be tested to determine whether the facts support or negate them. Obviously, the lower the decided likelihood of the event, the less the anxiety. But, again, this estimated likelihood must be believable and this is achieved only by basing it on evidence.

Before moving on to discuss how evidence is obtained, there is one other important point to make. It is much easier to obtain realistic evidence for a belief if it is clearly operationalized in its prediction. Evidence is very hard to obtain for vague, poorly defined beliefs. For example, a client may make a prediction that he is going to do very badly on an upcoming test. Rather than leaving the prediction in this vague form, you should ask the client to make more specific predictions about exactly what will go wrong. Let's say the client's prediction then becomes "I will fail." You need to find out what fail actually means—perhaps scoring less than 50 percent. This, then, is a much easier prediction to search for evidence on than a global thought such as "I will do badly," which is highly subjective.

There are many possible sources of evidence to examine. Obviously, what is examined will depend to some degree on the belief one is trying to find evidence for. Clients and therapists both need to allow themselves to be creative in coming up with evidence. There are some sources of evidence that are most commonly used and we will discuss them here.

Previous Experience

Clearly, one of the easiest sources of evidence for an individual to believe is his own prior experience. In most cases, the reality of what has happened previously is not nearly as bad as the prediction the individual makes. Therefore, simply stopping for a moment and reminding oneself of prior experience can often be of value.

However, there is one caveat. There is considerable evidence that anxious individuals tend to have a biased way of construing the world (see Dalgleish and Watts 1990). While current research does not seem to indicate a particular bias associated with recall (Rapee et al. 1993), there is evidence that anxious people pay excessive attention to threat cues and also interpret events as threatening (Asmundson and Stein 1994, Eysenck et al. 1991, Lucock and Salkovskis, 1988). As a result, recall may be distorted, especially in their tendency to remember events that support their belief (negative performance) and ignore or forget events that go against their beliefs (positive performance). You may find that your client recalls events from his past in a manner that indicates that his cumulative performance in a situation is worse than is actually the case. One way to avoid this is to teach clients to focus on the facts of the prior event rather than their overall evaluation (e.g., did he actually give the presentation versus how well he felt he performed). As discussed above, you will have encouraged your client to focus on clear, operationalized aspects of his belief. In the same way, he should be encouraged to focus on clear aspects of the prior experience (e.g. "Did you get less than 50 percent?", rather than "Did you do badly?"). Going one step further, you may sometimes wish to do more formal cognitive restructuring with some previous event that appears to have been misinterpreted and is part of the basis for the negative belief. Once restructured, this prior event can be used as evidence for future similar situations.

In those few cases where clients are unable to focus objectively on prior experience, you may need to abandon this form of evidence and focus on accumulating new evidence via hypothesis testing (see Chapter 8).

Objective Information

Another form of evidence involves having the client search for objective information regarding a particular belief. This information can come from newspapers, books, pamphlets, or even experts. For example, a female client who enjoys football might have a belief that watching football is a "man" thing. For homework, you might then set her the task of calling the marketing sections of several football teams and finding out as many facts as possible about the number of women interested in football.

Along similar lines, clients themselves can be encouraged to conduct their own surveys for certain information. For example, the female client mentioned above could be encouraged to attend a football game, pick a section of the crowd, and determine the proportion of women. This source of evidence is extremely useful for one of the fundamental fears in social phobia: the belief that "everyone is watching me." There is no doubt that you will have a client with this concern at some time. A particularly convincing procedure in this case is to have the client walk into various situations and actually count the number of people who are looking at him.

Asking Others

In addition to obtaining factual or expert information, clients should also be encouraged to solicit opinions from others. This latter source of information is often far more salient for social phobia than factual information. Of course, obtaining opinions from others generally requires a degree of ingenuity and there will be some circumstances where it is not possible. Difficulties involve the fact that seeking opinions about certain things can be socially inappropriate and also, given that people in our society often try to be polite, the client may not believe everything he is told. Nevertheless, there are many situations in which some clever lateral thinking can come up with ways of obtaining good information. This may involve techniques such as making up excuses for why you need the information or persuading a friend or partner to seek the information for you. For example, a client with social anxiety is feeling negative about himself because he was turned down for a date by a woman he was interested in. The client had the thought "I am a loser" following the incident. One useful exercise would be to have the client discuss the frequency of rejection among some of his friends so that he can develop a more realistic perspective about this occurrence and make a more appropriate evaluation of himself.

Putting Yourself in Another's Place

Probably the single most valuable source of evidence for an individual with social phobia is to learn to put himself in another person's position. Given that the major concern in social phobia is possible negative evaluation from others, it is extremely valuable for the individual to imagine what he would think if the situations were reversed. In many cases, he would not think badly of another person in the same situation and this should help demonstrate that others will in turn not think badly of him. Unfortunately, many clients with social phobia hold a double standard—they think others will evaluate them negatively for something despite the fact that they would not evaluate another person in that way for the same thing. This needs to be pointed out to clients and in some cases the illogicality of such a pattern will need to be extensively discussed. The technique of putting oneself in someone else's position may be best illustrated with an example.

THERAPIST: Tell me about this incident that's making you feel so uptight.

CLIENT: Well, I was introducing my cousin yesterday to a friend of mine and I got my cousin's name wrong. I quickly covered up, but I know he noticed because he tried to make a joke of it.

THERAPIST: That sounds like an awkward situation. You were saying before how embarrassed you felt. Why was that? What thoughts went through your head?

CLIENT: Oh, the immediate thought was, "He must think I'm so stupid." Then I lay awake last night thinking that he's never going to look at me in the same way again.

THERAPIST: OK, so you're thinking that your cousin must think you're stupid. By this, you seem to be implying 100 percent— that is, he must *definitely* think you're stupid.

CLIENT: Well, it's such a stupid thing to do. I know my cousin's name. Why would I get it wrong?

THERAPIST: Well, why don't we try and switch the situations around and see what you might think if this happened to you. Try to imagine that the situation happened in reverse. You were standing talking to your cousin when a friend of his came up to the two of you. Your cousin turned to the friend and said, "I would like to introduce my cousin, John . . . oh how stupid of me, I mean Jason." What would you think about your cousin?

CLIENT: Well, I would wonder why he got my name wrong.

THERAPIST: And your answer might be . . .

CLIENT: Obviously he knows who I am . . . so I guess perhaps he was distracted, or maybe he had the name John on his mind. I'm not really sure.

THERAPIST: Does it really matter? Has he done anything dreadful to you by getting your name wrong for a second?

CLIENT: No, not really.

THERAPIST: Most important, would you think he was stupid?

CLIENT: Of course not. He's a smart guy, my cousin.

THERAPIST: So, going back to the way the situation really happened, why should your cousin be so different from you? Why would he think you were stupid?

CLIENT: I guess he wouldn't.

THERAPIST: Let's think about one other thing. Imagine that you're back at the party. It's ten minutes later. You've spoken with several other people, you've listened to some music, perhaps you're eating or drinking. Would you still be thinking about your cousin forgetting your name?

CLIENT: Of course not, it would be long forgotten.

While most social phobics will believe that other people are critical, negative, or judgmental, this belief is generally held as an automatic assumption. Usually, once the belief is brought into consciousness, most social phobics will have the insight to realize the irrationality of it. Occasionally, however, some clients may actually believe that they are more sensitive, caring, or empathic than most other people in the world. In these cases, a client may admit that he wouldn't think badly of another in the same situation, but still not believe that this principle can then be applied back to the other person. In part, this is complicated by the selective attention people with social phobia apply to various situations. They tend to focus on critical people and as a result have an inflated sense of how many people are actually that way. While this degree of lack of insight is rare among most people with social phobia, it is difficult to deal with when it does exist. It may be possible to work on the insight gradually over the course of therapy, generally by using more direct sources of evidence to challenge this belief. For example, you may specifically target it by having your client ask people about their views on others' performance to demonstrate that they do not differ so much from his own. If you are not able to shift this belief (or until you do), it may be best to keep away from the use of "swapping positions" as a source of evidence.

Alternative Explanations

Finally, as indicated in the preceding example, encouraging your client to generate alternative possible explanations for events can also help to provide some perspective on the situation. For example, if a person were to smile while a client spoke to her, the client might immediately think "I must look silly." As evidence, the client should be encouraged to generate other possible reasons why the person may have been smiling. For example, she might have thought of something funny, she might herself have been shy, she might have been trying to be nice, and so forth. Remember that we are pushing *realistic* thinking here and not positive thinking. The purpose is not simply to replace one thought with another. This is not likely to be believed. Rather, by generating other plausible thoughts, the client should realize that the original belief is not necessarily 100 percent true; there are other possibilities, perhaps equally plausible, thus underscoring the shaky ground on which the client's negative thoughts rest.

As an example, one of us was recently treating a 15-year-old girl. She related an incident in which a boy she tried to speak to refused to say anything and simply walked away. Her belief was that he was snubbing her and did not like her from the outset. Through discussion, the therapist was able to help the client generate an alternative explanation: that the boy was himself shy and did not know how to speak to a 15-year-old girl. With two possible, equally plausible explanations, the client's anger and sadness over the incident did not disappear, but did reduce markedly. Interestingly, a few sessions later, we were discussing an incident in which the client had failed to speak to a boy at a party. When asked why, she said she wanted to, but had been "struck dumb" by her shyness. All of a sudden, she looked as though an enormous light bulb had gone off for her.

Step 3: Probabilities

Once all of the evidence has been evaluated, clients are in a position to determine the realistic probability with which their expectations will materialize. As we have been saying, when clients initially identify their prediction in a situation, it is most often associated with a 100 percent probability. For example, the belief, "They will laugh at me" assumes 100 percent, that is "They will *definitely* laugh at me." As stated earlier, the lower the evaluated probability of something negative happening, the lower will be the anxiety. But, as we have stressed, the client must believe his new estimate. That is, there must be concrete information available that the client believes supports the new estimate. Therefore, at this point, the client should summarize all of the evidence he has just gone through. Then basing his conclusions closely on the available evidence, he should come up with a *realistic* estimate of the likelihood that his initial prediction will occur.

Some clients will be able to work with real probabilities, that is, 100 percent, 50 percent, 1 percent, and so on. However, most clients will prefer to think in terms of qualitative descriptors, such as very likely, moderately likely, or extremely unlikely. It doesn't matter which is used and clients should be taught to go with whatever is comfortable. Again, the key is that it is realistic and that hopefully, it is less than the original assumption.

If we look at our overall goal of reducing anxiety and phobic behavior, any step resulting in a decrease in anxiety is a step in the right direction. At this point it becomes important to discuss with the client the importance of making gradual, systematic changes toward the overall goal. In this way you can dispel any notion that somehow a bolt of lightning will occur to eliminate all anxiety from the person's life.

John B.'s Example

Following coverage of the general principles of cognitive restructuring, John was asked to describe a recent event that had made him particularly nervous so that we could look at how he might have viewed it differently. John recalled an episode from a few days ago when he had to take his car to the mechanic for some repairs. At the time, he had been rather nervous before going and then had become extremely flustered when he began to tell the mechanic about the nature of the problem.

JOHN: As soon as the guy asked me to tell him what was wrong with the car, my mind went blank. I had real difficulty telling him what sort of sounds I heard and I couldn't remember the names of the engine parts. I just kept getting more and more nervous.

THERAPIST: Try to imagine that you're standing there trying to explain the problem. What was the main thought going through your mind?

JOHN: I'm not sure . . . I guess I was just wondering if I could get the car fixed.

THERAPIST: I'm sure you were. But *wondering* whether or not the car would be repaired is probably not going to make you very embarrassed. Why do you think you might have been getting so flustered? Did you expect that anything bad might happen in that situation?

JOHN: Well, I couldn't even remember the names of the car parts—and I'm generally pretty good with cars. I've been playing with them all my life. When my mind went blank, that just threw me. He must have really thought I was one of those rich jerks who never wants to get his hands dirty.

THERAPIST: So it sounds as though one of the main thoughts was "This guy thinks I'm a jerk."

JOHN: Yeah, I guess it would have been.

THERAPIST: OK, so there's your initial thought. When you say it like that, "The guy thinks I'm a jerk," it implies that it's definite—100 percent probability. The guy definitely thinks I'm a jerk.

JOHN: Well, when I couldn't even tell him where the trouble was, he must have.

THERAPIST: OK, now let's have a look at some of the evidence for that belief. How do you *know* that he thought you were a jerk? Did he say so? Did he give you an unpleasant look?

JOHN: No, he didn't do those things. But then, I'm the customer. He wouldn't do that.

THERAPIST: So at the moment, we have no reason to believe that he definitely did think you were a jerk. If you remember, another type of evidence we could look at is to think about whether there are any alternative possibilities. What are *all* the different things he might have thought?

JOHN: Hmm. I suppose he might have thought I was tired . . . it was pretty early in the morning . . . before work.

THERAPIST: Great. So it is possible that he might have thought you were a jerk, but it's also possible that he might have thought you were tired. What about just thinking that you weren't interested in cars?

JOHN: Yeah, possibly.

THERAPIST: OK, so earlier you thought that he *must* (100 percent) be thinking you're a jerk. Now, when we look at it more realistically, you can see that thinking you're a jerk is one possibility, but there are at least two others—that he thinks you're tired, or he thinks you're not interested in cars. There is probably an even better type of evidence to look at—trying to reverse positions.

JOHN: OK, how would I do that?

THERAPIST: Well, try to imagine that the shoe was on the other foot. Suppose this guy came into the post office and started asking you some questions about his mail and you realize that he doesn't have a clue about how the post office works. Would you think he was a jerk?

JOHN: Of course not. No one understands the mail system. I wouldn't think anything about him, I would just help him.

THERAPIST: Right. So why should things be so different the other way? It's his job to help you. He deals with all sorts of different people every day. So why should he pick you out and think that you're a jerk?

JOHN: Yeah, that's right. No reason I guess.

THERAPIST: Let's look at that in a different way. Imagine if you saw me dropping off my car at the shop. I don't know anything about cars. I'm sure that would be very clear to anyone if I tried to describe something that was wrong with my car. Would you think I was a jerk?

JOHN: No, I definitely wouldn't judge you in that situation.

THERAPIST: Hmm . . . why not? I'm a man and I appear to know nothing about cars. Isn't that the same information you're using to label yourself a jerk?

JOHN: I guess so, but when it applies to you, it doesn't seem to matter.

THERAPIST: Exactly. That's a perfect example of a double standard. If it applies to you, you think it's negative. If it applies to someone else, it doesn't matter.

OK. So let's try and put all that together. First, you have no direct reason to think that he thinks you're a jerk. He hasn't said anything or shown it in his face. Second, there are several realistic things that he might think about you—perhaps that you're tired or that you're just not interested in cars. And when you put yourself in his place, it really doesn't seem so very likely that he should think that you're a jerk. After all, you probably wouldn't do so in a reversed situation. Finally, not knowing about cars does not make someone a jerk.

So now I want you to run your mind back to the garage. Imagine yourself standing there and you get flustered and forget the names of some of the engine parts. Remind yourself of the evidence we just spoke about and work out how likely you think it really is that the mechanic will think you're a jerk.

JOHN: I guess when I look at all of those things, it really isn't very
  likely, is it?

Obviously, there is still quite a bit more you could do with this
belief. In particular, the next step would involve challenging the
consequences to the belief (decatastrophizing: So what if he did think
you were a jerk?). Hopefully John should be able to realize that even
if the mechanic did think he was a jerk, it's not a big deal. John is
not likely to see him again and he is of no great importance to John
in his life. However, at this stage, it is sufficient to work on this first
component of the technique in order for the client to become ac-
complished at evaluating evidence. The client first needs to be able
to challenge his own negative beliefs (probabilities) before he can
be confident enough not to be affected by other people's negative
evaluations if they did occur in that situation.

Homework

This is by no means the end of cognitive restructuring. In fact, cognitive restructuring will take place in and out of sessions from here
on. Practice and homework are essential. Each thought has to be
challenged, at times over and over again.

At this point, the client should understand how to identify an
underlying belief or assumption, to evaluate the evidence for this
assumption, and to estimate the realistic probability of its occurrence.
In the next session, clients will learn to evaluate the consequences
of their belief if it were to occur, and to distinguish between situations where other people's evaluations matter and where they don't.

For most clients cognitive restructuring is the most conceptually
difficult technique to grasp, and it will require a lot of work. Nevertheless, it is a vital component of treatment for social phobia and
therefore needs to be given considerable weight. For these reasons,
it is often a good idea to stop the session at this point and allow these
first components to sink in as well as to allow the client time to prac-

tice these initial steps. Some clients will be able to grasp these issues easily and, for them, you may wish to combine the two components of cognitive restructuring into a single session. Still others may have a great deal of difficulty and you may feel you need to divide the teaching of cognitive restructuring into even more components than we have done here. However, for most clients, it doesn't hurt to give them a week or more break before moving on to the next component of cognitive restructuring.

Homework should involve monitoring of beliefs and evidence. A suggested monitoring form is included Table 5–1 (an equivalent form is provided for clients in the client manual). You will need to go through this form in some detail with your client to ensure that he understands how to use it.

In the first column, *Event*, the client must include only external, factual items. Some clients will automatically interpret external events and will record these interpretations rather than the objective event itself. For example, a client who was giving a talk may record "gave bad talk." The term "bad" is a judgment and should be subject to evaluation of its evidence. By allowing it to enter the first column, it becomes seen as a given with 100 percent probability. Instead, this item should be entered as "gave talk" and an initial belief along the lines "I did a bad job" could go into the expectation column.

The second column is where the client should record the initial thought, belief, or assumption that was triggered by the event in column 1. It is labeled *Expectation* to remind the subject that he needs to record a statement of what he predicts or expects will happen in the situation. It is assumed that most expectations in this column will be associated with an unstated 100 percent probability.

The next step is for the client to evaluate the evidence for this prediction. All assessed evidence should be recorded in the third column, labeled *Evidence*. Then, based on an amalgam of the evaluated evidence, the client should determine the realistic *Probability* (fourth column) that the outcome predicted in column 2 will occur.

Table 5–1. Realistic thinking form—1.

Event	Expectation (Initial prediction)	Evidence (How do I know)	Probability (Realistic)	Degree of Emotion (0–8)

Finally, he should rate his anxiety or embarrassment in column 5 once the realistic probability of the prediction is taken into account. This rating should be made using the 0–8 scale from the Social Situations Record (p. 40). Presumably, if the realistic probability is lower than the original, assumed probability (less than 100 percent), and it is believed, the embarrassment should be less than it was originally. However, it should be pointed out to clients that it is very unlikely that anxiety will decrease to 0. In fact, until the client becomes practiced at the technique and also adds in the later components, there may be little effect on anxiety at all. In the beginning stages we reinforce the client for doing the exercise and try not to get too caught up in whether it is working. Ultimately, if practiced and done correctly, it will have an effect, but it may take a while. Of course, a little extra encouragement may be needed in the early stages, before the technique begins to work.

It is also important to note that this rating of emotion may be quite meaningless and difficult for clients when the form is being used to practice cognitive restructuring for hypothetical or retrospective events. In these cases, the client might try to rate what he thinks his emotion would have been if he had restructured as practiced, or this rating could be left out. The emotion rating will make the most sense and be most useful when using the forms for current or upcoming events.

As with all of our techniques, practice is the key to success. It is rare for clients to get cognitive restructuring right at first, so it is vital that they practice frequently before the next meeting with you so that you can see all of the difficulties with the technique and help to correct them. In addition, extensive use of the forms will help to reveal more of the clients' cognitive distortions. The homework for this stage is simply to use the monitoring form to practice cognitive restructuring as often as possible. Because many clients do not routinely experience high levels of anxiety frequently (in part because of avoidance behavior), we generally suggest that they begin by recording any episode in which they experience anxiety, even if it is only to a mild degree. In fact, the same principles of cognitive restructuring can be applied to other emotions, such as anger or depression, and so, for the sake of practice, clients can be urged to record all negative emotional episodes. It should be stressed that the purpose at this stage is not to reduce anxiety but to practice identifying beliefs and evaluating evidence. Therefore, they do not need to work on only serious instances of anxiety but should begin to identify any level for the sake of practice. You may want to brainstorm a few examples with your client, since some clients assume that the term *anxiety* refers only to intense affect. One advantage of starting with low level anxiety situations is that it is easier for the client to learn the process, as high levels of anxiety are often more difficult to challenge. If you conceptualize cognitive restructuring as a skill, then beginning with low-level situations will allow the client to practice the skill under the least difficult circumstances.

Given that it is often impractical for clients to record their restructuring on the spot, they should be encouraged to use the monitoring form as soon as possible after an event. However, whenever possible, completing the form on the spot is more useful. The value of carrying the form with them at all times should be stressed. Since clients with social anxiety tend to be self-conscious, you may need to restructure thoughts about the likelihood of someone seeing the client recording. However, since practice is so vital, even if they forget to do their monitoring at the moment, thinking back over the events of the day and doing some monitoring in the evening is a good idea. While it is true that the situation and feeling are likely to have passed by that time, the procedure will still have therapeutic value in that the client will be restructuring thoughts and beliefs that will come up again. Thus, each time these thoughts are dealt with, their strength will decrease and more realistic thoughts will begin to become more automatic. Of course, the ideal time to implement the cognitive restructuring technique is when there are impending events the client is worried about. In this case, restructuring would focus on thoughts related to the anticipatory anxiety. The client should complete the form ahead of time and, presumably, this will prime his realistic thinking when the situation actually occurs, in addition to reducing anticipatory anxiety.

Dealing with Difficulties

There are several difficulties that you may come across with this component of cognitive restructuring.

Inability to Identify Beliefs

Some clients will experience great difficulty in identifying their initial beliefs or predictions. They may report such comments as, "I don't have thoughts in these situations—I just feel." In these cases, it is important to go back over the rationale and examples and make sure that the client at least agrees in principle that underlying beliefs are mediating his feelings. If a client does not agree with this principle in theory (perhaps a valid point!), then you may be able to reach a compromise position where he agrees that beliefs can often influence our feelings, even if they are not always the final cause. That is, even if a feeling does not always stem from cognitions, thoughts will still have an impact on the feeling once it is triggered. You should also go back over the discussion of automatic thoughts and make sure that the client understands that his beliefs will not always be available to consciousness.

In most cases, clients should be encouraged to keep practicing. Continued practice will usually help people to begin to identify their underlying beliefs. This can also be facilitated by regular discussions with you, the therapist. Clients should discuss events, past and present, that caused them anxiety, and you can help to identify possible underlying beliefs via questioning and brainstorming. Finally, in those few cases where a client just cannot identify thoughts, he should be encouraged to work with hypotheticals. That is, he should generate a belief that he might possibly hold in a situation that could lead to anxiety. For example, a person who experiences public speaking anxiety but cannot identify thoughts about it can generate hypothetical cognitions such as "I am worried people will not be interested in what I have to say," or "I will forget my presentation." He should then go through the process of evaluating evidence for this thought and come up with a realistic probability. Next, he should go on to make up another possible belief, and so on. By realizing that there is little evidence for any potential negative outcome, clients can often reduce their anxiety without necessarily being able to point to the specific thought that they held.

Highly Unstructured Clients

Most clients have difficulty doing cognitive restructuring at first. However, at times you may come across a client who has even more difficulty, largely because he is too unstructured in his thinking to follow the procedure. In general, this type of client can be helped by longer practice periods scheduled in therapy and by your imposing a very tight structure onto the procedure. For example, you might break the process down into a number of set steps, each with a short label, and you might ask the client to learn these labels by rote, in order. You might want to make a list of questions a client should be asking himself to facilitate cognitive restructuring, rather than relying on him to come up with his own.

However, the thinking of some clients may be so abstract that they really cannot learn the procedure as structured above. This may also apply to clients with intellectual difficulties. In these cases, it may be best to switch to a different cognitive restructuring procedure. Rather than the Beck approach advocated here, one similar to Donald Meichenbaum's (1977) might be a better alternative. The broad principle of this latter approach is to simply insert alternate beliefs, following identification of negative ones. In other words, rather than using an empirical challenge to beliefs, clients are simply taught a set of positive coping self-statements to use in place of their irrational ones. For example, if a client was worried about writing in front of another person, he might be taught simply to say to himself, "I know I can do this without shaking," or "It doesn't matter if I shake in front of this person," and so on. Naturally, the difficulty here is the issue of belief. However, you may be surprised at how often clients, especially intellectually disabled ones, benefit from this procedure as it allows them to focus their attention on more functional cognitions, even if not self-generated.

Ultimately, if cognitive restructuring does not work with a particular client, there are other techniques, and it may be best to simply let it go.

Judgmental Clients

Occasionally you may come across a client who is himself very judgmental or critical. As a result, there will be an assumption that "other people think like me." Clearly, such a client is not a candidate for the method of evaluating evidence that involves putting himself in someone else's shoes. However, other forms of evidence evaluation should be of value. If the judgmental attitudes continue to get in the way, it may become necessary to take some time in therapy to explore these beliefs. Some discussion of their origins, the "value" of holding onto them, and the rights of others may help.

Failure to Really Appreciate Probabilities

Finally, some clients will have difficulty fully appreciating the meaning of probabilities. For example, a client might agree, after examination of the evidence, that there is very little chance that someone will laugh at him in a particular situation. However, he might still report considerable anxiety because "*any* chance is still too much." Such conservativeness—not accepting any possibility of a negative occurrence—is not uncommon in highly anxious individuals and can interfere with treatment. It may be important for you to take some time to discuss the pros and cons of living life with some risk as opposed to trying to avoid all risks in life. Pointing out the tremendous restrictions caused by the social phobia and putting low probabilities into perspective can help. For example, you can ask whether he would never drive because of the risk of a car accident, or whether he would buy a new house on the assumption of winning the lottery. Both are possible but improbable, and are unlikely to have a strong impact on his behavior. In other words, sometimes people are willing to superficially acknowledge low probabilities for danger, but they may not truly realize what this means or understand all of the implications.

6

⚘

Cognitive Restructuring—II

AIMS

1. Discussing homework.
2. Continuing cognitive restructuring—catastrophic outcomes.

Discussion of Homework

It is vital to ensure that your client has monitored a number of anxiety-provoking situations throughout the intervening period between sessions. As mentioned earlier, it is the exceptional client who will have no difficulties with monitoring cognitions in the beginning. Therefore, you will need to spend a large proportion of this session discussing each recorded event with your client. Difficulties the client had should be used to illustrate her typical thinking style and you should then take the opportunity to initiate questions that will guide her to discover the irrationality of these beliefs, where appropriate. For each belief, you should ask in detail about the basis for the thought and the evidence the client used to challenge that belief. You may find that some clients will regularly rely on a particular type of evidence, and most will fail to examine all potential sources of evidence. This is not necessarily a problem, as long as the client manages to convince herself that her estimated probabilities are too high. Nevertheless, at times you may be able to suggest additional sources of evidence to provide your client with a wider range of options. In addition, the more evidence provided to refute the belief, the more likely you are to get substantial and lasting anxiety reduction.

Cognitive Restructuring—Catastrophic Outcomes

As we have previously seen, empirical evidence supports the suggestion that people with social phobia tend to overestimate the likelihood that negative events will occur in social/evaluative situations. There is also evidence that these people overestimate the consequences of these negative events, in other words, how negative they will be. In a study by Butler and Mathews (1983), not only did anxious subjects rate negative events as more likely to occur to them than did nonanxious subjects, but they also rated these events as being more negative. In the case of social phobia, a 1996 study by Edna Foa and colleagues (described earlier) has shown that changing subjects' estimates of the consequences of negative social events was the best predictor of the degree to which they improved in treatment.

Most people don't have a single belief about a situation, but have a series of beliefs, each stemming from the previous one, like the layers of an onion. One follows the other as an assumed consequence. In other words, people often think along the lines of "If such and such happens, then such and such will follow." In most cases, not only is the original belief an overestimate of the likelihood of its occurrence, but the second belief is also an exaggeration. For example, an individual may think, "I will make a mistake here and then people will laugh at me." In this case, the belief, "I will (definitely) make a mistake" is most likely an exaggerated probability. Similarly, the belief "people will laugh at me" is also an exaggeration. Beck refers to this as *catastrophic thinking* and it is probably one of the most detrimental thinking styles common to all anxiety disorders. The treatment for catastrophic thinking follows directly from the previous work on cognitive restructuring.

As usual, it is best to begin with a rationale for this next stage of the program. A discussion of the role of catastrophic thinking should be sufficient because most clients will recognize this style very quickly. Ask your client to provide examples from her life. Most clients will have several. If your client cannot for some reason produce any examples, you should point out some of the ones you have observed. If this is not possible, then generation of some typical catastrophic beliefs reported by people with social phobia should ring some bells.

Once the client understands the theory behind catastrophic thinking, the next step simply involves continuing the cognitive restructuring exercise from the previous session. By now your client should be able to identify an initial belief and its realistic probability of occurrence. The next step is asking the client to imagine that the event she was expecting actually did occur. She should then try to imagine what the consequence of that event would be. We generally suggest to our clients to use the phrases, "so what" or "what if." For example, the client's first thought might be "I will make a mistake." She should then ask herself, "So what (or what would happen) if I did make a mistake?" The rules for this next belief should be very similar to the rules for the initial belief—that is, the belief should be phrased as a statement of expectation and should not be an emotion. For example, many clients will be tempted to come up with the consequence "That would be terrible." But they should then be encouraged to ask themselves "Why would it be terrible? What would *actually* happen?"

When clients generate a consequence, either of two broad scenarios might arise. Sometimes, they may generate a consequence that is either totally ludicrous or neutral. In this case, anxiety would drop to 0 (or close) and the exercise is over. For example, the client may think "they will pelt me with stones," and will then laugh, presumably because she instantly realizes that the probability of this is 0. Alternately, the consequence may be something along the lines "If I make a mistake, then my supervisor will correct it," or "I can handle that," or "that would be fine," and so on, and there is no further work to do.

More commonly, clients will generate a consequence that is truly catastrophic. For example, "everyone will laugh at me," or "everyone will hate me." In this case, the consequence can be treated in exactly the same way as the previous initial belief. That is, it can be conceptualized as an overestimated probability and can then be subjected to an evaluation of evidence. For example, a client may perceive the consequence, "everyone will laugh at me." You might then ask, "How do you know that everyone will laugh at you?" The client might look at previous experience, putting herself in another's position, and so on. She should then be in a position to determine a realistic probability for this belief. In most cases, there will be yet another catastrophic consequence to this second belief. This also needs to be identified and its evidence evaluated. This procedure should continue until there is a logical end.

A so-called "logical end" to a cognitive restructuring exercise can take several forms and there is no one correct way to end. The main objective is for the client to begin to shift her extreme beliefs in a more realistic direction and, as a result, is able to reduce her social fear and levels of anxiety. An obvious end to the procedure is if a client reaches zero probability for an outcome. Nevertheless, there may be some circumstances in which you might wish to look hypothetically at the next consequence, even when the previous belief had a zero likelihood. For example, suppose a client is worried about crossing lanes in front of someone while driving in traffic. You might determine that a lower-level belief is that "the driver behind will hate me." Looking at the evidence, the client might then decide that in fact there is no probability at all that the driver will hate her. Nevertheless, you might wish to get your client to explore the consequence of "so what if this total stranger does decide that she hates you?" Your client might then work out the facts that she doesn't know this other driver, the other driver doesn't know her, and they will probably never meet. Therefore, going a step further in this circumstance might just help to reinforce the innocuousness of the whole situation even more.

In other situations, the end of the procedure might come when the client can think of no further consequences. Many clients will often reach a consequence that can be described as their "basic belief." Basic beliefs are broad truisms of life that underlie many of an individual's motivations and, in a sense, drive their feelings. They are very similar to what Ellis and Harper (1975) describe as "common irrational beliefs." Some basic beliefs might include "it is essential to be liked by everyone," "I must never make mistakes," or "I must never get into trouble." Often, an individual will be guided largely by one basic belief, although sometimes there may be several. Once a client identifies a basic belief, she is likely to come across this same belief in a majority of her cognitive restructuring tasks. In this case, it will be very important to deal with and restructure this belief so that once it is correctly restructured, it can serve as the end point of the exercise and the client will immediately realize its irrationality. In addition, in cases where a common basic belief mediates a majority of an individual's concerns, this can begin to serve as a shortcut for cognitive restructuring, a point that will be discussed in more detail later.

Restructuring a basic belief may sometimes be a difficult task, although surprisingly often it is relatively simple. In many cases, the basic belief is clearly unrealistic and, once identified, is easily shifted. For example, a belief such as "everyone must like me" is clearly not possible and the majority of clients who identify such beliefs will immediately realize this. As we explain to clients, the reason the belief has lasted so long and has been so influential in their behavior is precisely because it is automatic and has been left unchallenged. Basic beliefs are implicit truths. Without being challenged they persist.

In some cases, basic beliefs are not so clearly irrational and may be harder (or even impossible) to shift. Often these are overarching life scripts for the individual (fundamental beliefs by which she lives her life, and may be rooted in religious convictions, cultural tenets, or messages received from parents. When you identify this type of underlying belief and it seems to dominate a large proportion of the person's life, it may be a good idea to take some time out from the set program and spend a session or two discussing this particular life script. It is often useful for the individual to discuss issues such as where the message came from, what effects it is having on the individual's life, what evidence there is for the belief, how many other people may hold these beliefs, and how other people may cope with similar beliefs. Helping the individual to develop insight into the belief may allow her to change it or let it go, or, if this is not possible, may at least help her to identify adaptive ways of coping or living with it. For example, a female client of Arabic descent had several fears related to the possibility of making mistakes at work. She was able to reduce these fears to some extent by examining the probabilities and realizing that she was good at her job and was unlikely to make mistakes. However, some fear remained. When cognitive restructuring was used to examine some of the consequences, it eventually became clear that at the bottom of the various fears was the belief that women should not work. The client recognized that this belief was an integral aspect of her traditional culture and she did not think that it was irrational. A session was spent helping the client to explore all of the sources and implications of this belief. At the end, the client was not able to reconcile the clash between her traditional culture and her new culture, but by bringing all of the issues into the open, a large part of the anxiety was reduced.

Short Cuts to Cognitive Restructuring

It will take the average client considerable practice to master this procedure. To encourage mastery, you should go through as many examples with the client in therapy sessions as time permits. Different clients will require more or less help. Ideally, the examples in session should be ones that are real for the client, preferably current situations from her life, and you should try to spell out the entire procedure as often as possible in writing, either on a monitoring form, or on a board. Although this may seem tedious, it is the best way for clients to begin to internalize the procedure, and make their realistic beliefs more automatic.

Once you feel that the client is becoming better at the procedure (often after a few weeks), you may suggest that she begin to reduce the complexity of the technique. At first, this might involve simply identifying a series of beliefs and then reminding herself of the evidence, rather than having to generate it over and over. Later, the client should be able to jump straight to one or two key beliefs in a given situation (e.g., "they are all staring at me") and evaluate one or two key pieces of evidence (e.g., "I don't usually stare at people walking down the street"). In many cases, the key belief will be the person's basic belief. Clients with prominent basic beliefs may well find that they can reduce their anxiety simply by reminding themselves of the irrationality of their basic belief, rather than going over each of the specific thoughts that stem from it. These short cuts can make the cognitive restructuring procedure much faster and more portable. However, it is important to remind the client that this can only happen once she is well practiced in the procedure, once she has begun to notice repetitive patterns in her thinking, and once she has repeatedly looked at the realistic evidence and convinced herself of the irrationality of many of her beliefs. Clients should be encouraged to stick with the full procedure for several weeks until the information elicited from the procedure becomes relatively automatic.

John B.'s Example

In one of the early sessions with John, a particularly good example for cognitive restructuring came up. A woman had come into the post office, very irate about the fact that her mail had been dropped on the ground. The boss had asked John to speak with her. John's initial thought was "I will say the wrong thing."

THERAPIST: OK, John, now you are starting to become better at the cognitive restructuring. Why don't you begin by looking at evidence from previous experiences?

JOHN: I haven't really had many like this. I generally manage to get out of dealing with the public. I can only remember one time when a man came in who was very angry about something, but I can't remember what. And the boss told me to handle it.

THERAPIST: What happened that time?

JOHN: I more or less froze. I didn't know what to say, so most of the time I just sat there. Finally, I think I said a few meaningless things and he finally left.

THERAPIST: Did he still seem angry when he left or was he more relaxed?

JOHN: No, he wasn't angry. In fact, he seemed to think that I had helped in some way, but I really didn't do anything.

THERAPIST: Well, often one of the best ways to deal with anger is simply to listen. It sounds as though you actually did a great job. So your one experience with an angry member of the public was actually a positive one.

JOHN: I guess it was. But I haven't done it much, so I still wouldn't know what to say.

THERAPIST: Yes, that's true. What about other bits of evidence? Are you generally a sensitive person? Are you usually OK with words?

JOHN: No, I'm usually pretty bad with words. I don't really have many friends so I don't get much chance to practice. But I am pretty sensitive. After all, when you have a problem like mine, you become pretty understanding of what people can go through.

THERAPIST: OK, so putting that evidence together—you haven't had much experience with words or with angry customers. But your one prior experience with an angry person worked out well and you are sensitive to other people's feelings. What do you think the realistic probability is that you will say the wrong thing?

JOHN: Maybe 50/50?

THERAPIST: I personally think that's still pretty high because if you are a generally sensitive person, it's pretty hard to say the wrong thing. But let's go with that—it's certainly not 100 percent likely. Now let's imagine that you did actually say the wrong thing. What would happen then?

JOHN: Well, the customer would get angry at me.

THERAPIST: Perhaps she would—and then so what? What would happen if she did get angry at you? [Note: At this point the therapist jumped immediately to the next consequence because he realized that the likelihood that the client would get angry at John if John did say the wrong thing was probably quite high. If John had been doing this exercise himself on his monitoring sheets, he should have gone through this step and discovered this for himself.]

JOHN: Well, no one wants someone to get angry at them.

THERAPIST: You're right, we usually don't. But at times all of us do something that makes another person angry and most of us usually don't avoid it at all costs. Why are you so desperate to avoid this person getting angry at you? What would really happen if she did?

JOHN: I don't really know. It would just be terrible.

THERAPIST: Would she hit or injure you?

JOHN: No, and I could protect myself if she tried.

THERAPIST: Then what? Could it be that you think she wouldn't like you?

JOHN: Yeah, maybe. Sure, if she got angry at me, she wouldn't like me.

THERAPIST: Well, let's look at the evidence for this belief. I think the best evidence in this case would be to put yourself in her place and think about your prior experience. Can you remember a time when you got angry at someone?

JOHN: Sure. I got really furious at a guy in a store a few months back.

THERAPIST: And how did you feel about him after? How do you feel about him now? Do you really hate him?

JOHN: Of course not. I haven't thought about him for months. I don't really feel any way about him. In fact, I realized the next day, when I calmed down, that some of it was my fault. Yeah, I guess you're right. She would probably just forget about me fairly soon after.

THERAPIST: OK, let's take it one step further. Let's assume that she didn't like you. What would happen then? Do you know her? Did she ever like you? Have you lost anything?

JOHN: Looking at it like that, it really doesn't matter that much, does it? She's just some person from out there. I've never seen her before and probably will never see her again. But no one wants to think people are walking around not liking them, do they?

THERAPIST: Sure. I certainly don't. But remember there's a difference between realistic and excessive. It's not pleasant to think that there's anyone around who doesn't like you. That's why we generally try to be pleasant to people. But it's not the end of the world if there is and it's quite unrealistic to expect that we will never be disliked. If this became a pattern—that is, if you had several people angry at you, then we would have to consider that a problem may exist that we have to deal with in a different way. However, if in all the years that you've been working, you've only had two instances where people have gotten angry at you, this hardly sounds like a pattern. Think of all the people you've dealt with during that time. Do you ever give yourself credit for dealing acceptably with them?

JOHN: Yeah, I've never thought of it that way. I guess I can go with that.

THERAPIST: OK, we've talked about a lot here. Let's recap. The bottom line is that the very worst that could happen if you were to say the wrong thing to the angry customer would be that she doesn't like you. And when you look at all of the evidence, that isn't very likely anyway, nor is it all that likely that you would say the wrong thing in the first place.

Homework

Homework from this session is quite simply to practice the expanded cognitive restructuring procedure. A sample monitoring form (Table 6–1) is included on p. 86. This now includes an additional column for recording expected *consequences*. Thus, after the client has recorded the realistic probability and current emotion, she should go on to ask herself the question, "What would happen if the expected outcome actually did occur?" She should then record this consequence in the appropriate column. It is extremely important to point out to clients that the procedure does not end there. The recorded consequence should then be repeated in the expectation column below the initial belief. This then allows evaluation (and recording) of the evidence, the realistic probability, and the subsequent consequence, and so on. The analogy of the layers of an onion is a useful one. Clients need to keep spiraling down to deeper and deeper beliefs. It is quite possible for a client to fill in two or three pages of monitoring for a single cognitive restructuring instance. This is a very difficult concept for many clients who often have a tendency to stop at the first level. Repeated practice and shaping by the therapist are important. A sample form, as completed by John B. in the example just discussed, is given in Table 6–2.

It is also a good idea to remind your client when to practice the technique. Again, as described in the previous session, she should

Table 6–1. Realistic thinking form—2.

Event	Expectation (Initial prediction)	Evidence (How do I know)	Probability (Realistic)	Emotion (0–8)	Consequence (What if)

Table 6-2. Sample realistic thinking form showing John's example.

Event	Expectation (Initial prediction)	Evidence (How do I know?)	Probability (Realistic)	Emotion (0–8)	Consequence (What if)
Having to deal with angry woman	I will say the wrong thing	Managed to handle anger once before Generally sensitive and understanding	50%	4	She will get angry at me
	She will get angry at me She won't like me	I don't dislike everyone I get angry at She will probably forget me altogether	Very likely Very little	4 1	She won't like me Doesn't really matter

try to do the restructuring immediately in any anxiety-provoking situation if possible. If this is not possible, she should do it as soon as possible after. However, if it is not done then, it should still be done in retrospect that night or the next day, purely as practice. Practicing afterwards will prime the generation of a realistic response at a later time.

DEALING WITH DIFFICULTIES

Several Beliefs

Sometimes clients will report several beliefs flooding into their minds simultaneously when entering a situation. This is not a problem. It simply requires the client to address each one in a systematic fashion. She should pick the most pressing belief (or any belief at random if she can't decide) and should deal completely with that one first. Often the other beliefs will arise as consequences of the first one and will thus be dealt with along the way. If not, she simply moves onto the next separate belief after dealing with the first. In other words, it is quite possible to have more than one cognitive restructuring exercise for a single evaluative situation.

Dependent Probabilities

Dependent probability is the term we use to refer to the fact that the probability of occurrence of a consequence is dependent on the probability of the occurrence of the belief before it. While this sounds a bit like a confusing law of physics, it is in fact quite simple. Let's suppose we have two beliefs: an initial belief (belief 1), and then a second belief, which is identified as a consequence (belief 2). If a client decides that the realistic probability of belief 1 is 10 percent and the realistic probability of its consequence is 50 percent, then the actual probability of belief 2 occurring at all is 5 percent—that is, 50 percent of 10 percent. This is because belief 2 only occurs *if belief 1 occurs* (a 10 percent chance). For example, Sally is going to a party. Her initial thought is "no one will speak to me." After looking at all the evidence, she decides that there is realistically only a 1 percent chance that *no one* will speak to her. She then looks at what would happen if no one did speak to her. Her second belief is "I would look very silly." After looking at the evidence she decides that there is a 10 percent chance that she will look silly if no one speaks to her. At this point, she becomes worried because she thinks that her probabilities are going up, from 1 percent to 10 percent. But, in fact, Sally needs to realize that the probability that she will look very silly is *dependent* on the chance that no one will speak to her. If someone speaks to her, suddenly she looks fine. Therefore, the actual probability that she will look very silly is 10 percent of 1 percent—in other words, very, very little!

You may come across clients from time to time who have great difficulty with this concept. They will treat each consequent belief as a separate entity. As a result, if the probability for any one of these "lower" beliefs goes up, they will begin to think that there is now a high chance of something going wrong, and their anxiety will increase. It is very important in these cases to try to point out or illustrate the above principles. Otherwise, the procedure will most likely not work.

7

✺

Attention Training

AIMS

1. Understanding the rationale of attentional focus.
2. Learning attention-strengthening exercises.
3. Applying what has been learned.

Rationale

Attentional training for social phobia is the newest of the procedures described in this program. You will not find mention of it in most current empirically tested programs for social phobia. Nevertheless, it is a technique that is beginning to be discussed with respect to social phobia and some case studies demonstrating its value are beginning to appear (Ribordy et al. 1981, Ziegler 1994).

The use of attentional training in the management of social anxiety is a direct prediction from the model presented earlier in this book. According to the model, one of the maintaining factors in social phobia is a tendency to focus excessive attentional resources onto indications of threat (i.e., negative evaluation from others such as frowns or yawns) and one's mental representation of how one appears to others. This focus comes at the expense of paying attention to necessary functions, such as the task one is performing. As a result, performance is often compromised and anxiety is increased. Therefore, the purpose of attentional training is to teach clients to focus their attention away from unnecessary or detrimental areas toward more valuable ones.

The rationale provided to clients should cover the above information at an appropriate level. In addition, you should discuss some obvious examples from the client's own experience. Most clients will be able to recall times when their performance in a situation was especially poor because they were concentrating more on what others were thinking of them or how they looked than on what they were supposed to be doing. For example, while telling a joke, a client may have forgotten the punchline, or when introducing someone, may have forgotten his name, or when working with someone looking over his shoulder, may have made some elementary mistakes.

Attention Strengthening

While it is probably not necessary for all clients, most would probably benefit from spending a few weeks learning to strengthen their powers of attention. This could have the dual benefit of improving the client's ability to shift and maintain attentional focus and increasing his confidence in his ability to do so.

Attention strengthening refers to any procedure in which the client is taught to sustain attention for increasing lengths of time. Generally, the task should be a relatively mundane one where there is some obvious indication of whether attention is maintained or not. Examples could include reading relatively uninteresting passages from books or magazines, crossing out particular letters from written passages, doing long crossword puzzles, or doing pages of mental arithmetic. You and your client can be creative in coming up with alternatives. In each case your client needs to practice performing the task for increasing periods of time, not letting his attention wander away from it. Each time his attention does wander, he needs to simply bring it back to the task and continue. With practice, he should find that he is able to concentrate for increasing periods of time without having his attention wander.

We usually also teach our clients a simple meditation technique. This follows the basic lines advocated by Herbert Benson (1976). Meditation is a convenient, portable procedure that encourages strengthening of attentional focus and can also be used as an effective form of relaxation. As a result, clients derive a dual benefit.

Any meditational or relaxation procedure can be used. Research does not indicate any particular differences among them. The one we use most often relies on the client matching counting to his breathing. The person should relax all his muscles and get into a smooth, regular rate of breathing. Then, on each inhalation, he should count (mentally) and visualize the number "one" and on exhalation, say and visualize the word "relax." The exercise can either be repeated in this way—"one-relax," over and over—or counting can continue— "two, three, four, etc." on each successive breath. We generally recommend going as far as "ten" and then returning to the beginning to remove any competitive emphasis from the exercise. In other words, many clients will feel driven to do better and better each day and will miss the point of the procedure due to this competition with themselves. Most important, clients should be instructed to try to maintain attentional focus onto the words and numbers and away from extraneous thoughts. Each time an extraneous thought comes into their heads, attention should be brought back to the counting and it should start again.

Practice needs to be relatively easy to begin with. It should be done in a quiet room with the phone off the hook and all distractions removed. As clients improve, practice should be made increasingly difficult. Gradually more and more distractions can be added to the situation, just like adding weights in weight training. For example, practice can be done with eyes open, lights on, and eventually with the radio or TV going.

One of the values of the procedure is that it can be practiced at home on a regular basis, but can also be practiced in a variety of situations. Clients should be encouraged to practice for brief periods whenever they have a chance, for example, standing on line, ignoring the commercials on TV, and even sitting on the toilet. This will enable clients to be more prepared to use the technique when needed. More detail about the procedure is given in the client manual.

Application

Attentional focus simply involves teaching clients the principles of the procedure and then encouraging them to try it in social situations. For some clients, this is all they need. They may never before have thought about their performance difficulties from this perspective and, when they put it into practice, it may be like a light going on in their heads. Others will understand the principles but will require several weeks of attentional training exercises to develop both the attentional control and the confidence to use the procedure. Finally, there will be some clients for whom this procedure just does not make sense.

Clients need to be instructed in the idea that when they are in a social situation, their attention should be focused onto the other person when he is speaking and then switched to their own message when they themselves are speaking. They need to become more aware of the "wrong" areas for their attention to focus, such as what others might be thinking, the redness or heat in their face, their posture, others' facial expressions, and so on. They need to consciously try to focus their attention away from these "wrong" areas and onto the task at hand. To a large degree, the ability to do this rests on the effective use of cognitive restructuring. To focus away from the threat cues requires that they no longer find them as anxiety provoking and that therefore they require less attention. Discussion of several hypothetical situations or prior examples may be of value. In addition, it may be useful to practice doing some role play (See chapter 9). During the role play you can encourage your client to try to focus his attention onto different areas and see what happens to his anxiety level and performance.

Homework

Homework for this section is practicing the attentional training procedures. If the client is doing the meditation, we generally recommend practice twice a day for around ten minutes each time. Use of a monitoring form is helpful to encourage regular practice and to give you an indication of what is happening. Additional "mini-practices" should not be forgotten.

Finally, the client can also be encouraged to practice applying the technique in naturally occurring situations and report on his experiences. However, set practices can wait until in vivo exposure is instituted (see Chapter 8).

8

Exposure

AIMS

1. Providing the rationale and theory of exposure.
2. Developing an exposure hierarchy.
3. Beginning exposure exercises.

Exposure is simply a procedure in which the individual comes into contact with (or confronts) the situation/event/activity that she fears. Many different techniques come under this broad category: systematic desensitization, paradoxical intention, graduated exposure, flooding. All share the same basic principle—bringing the client into contact with the feared event—and differ with respect to the method of delivery of this principle as well as additional bells and whistles. Many researchers argue that the therapeutic effects are caused by the basic exposure aspects of each technique and that the bells and whistles simply make the procedure more palatable for the client. Certainly, empirical studies rarely show large differences among any of these procedures. For more information about the theories of exposure or empirical findings, see Barlow (1988), Foa and McNally (1996), and Williams (1996).

Exposure is the fundamental treatment technique for all anxiety disorders. If you examine virtually any successful treatment package for anxiety, you will find some component that can be broadly labeled exposure. Even Freud argued that to deal fully with neurotic anxiety, a person must be encouraged to confront the situations she fears. Therefore, this next component will be the one where you and your client will really begin to notice some gains. However, significant and rapid gains will come only if your client has already developed some basic coping strategies in the form of cognitive restructuring and attentional training. In an excellent demonstration of this principle, Mattick and colleagues (1989) treated three groups of social phobics. One group received cognitive restructuring only, another received exposure only, and the third received a combination of the two. The group that received only cognitive restructuring showed few gains at the end of treatment. However, they did improve rapidly after treatment, most likely because they were now confident enough to enter previously feared situations, thus accomplishing their own exposure. The group that received only exposure improved markedly throughout treatment. However, they were more likely to relapse after treatment had finished, probably because they did not have the coping ability and attitude change to continue to apply their skills. The only group that showed consistent improvement both during and following treatment was the one that received combined treatment.

Rationale

It is important to provide a good rationale to your clients because, as one would expect, exposure is often an unpleasant procedure. After all, they are being asked to actually do all of the things they have spent the better part of their lives trying not to do! It's like going to the dentist—no one wants to do it, but we will do it if we think it is worthwhile. Therefore, convincing your client that exposure is worthwhile will help you tremendously in gaining her cooperation. In most cases this is not very difficult because exposure is a fundamentally commonsense procedure. In fact, we usually sell it to our clients in this way by telling them that we will not be doing anything magical or mysterious with them, but will be asking them to do a very logical procedure which will not be easy, but will be very beneficial.

Most clients will be familiar with the age-old advice: if you fall off your bike, get straight back on it. It should not be too hard to convince people that confronting their fears will be beneficial. In fact, you will probably find that many of your clients have tried something similar themselves.

In giving a rationale, we generally try to provide clients with a common example from daily life. There are many examples you could use. The main idea is to illustrate the principle that if an individual repeatedly spends time in a feared situation, the anxiety gradually diminishes, as it allows her to disconfirm her feared consequences. Examples might include infants going into the sea for the first time, learning to drive, a teacher on her first assignment, and so on. Once you have gone through an example like this, you might ask your client to generate some more basic examples from her own life. These examples could be activities your client is now able to do with little thought, but which at one time produced considerable anxiety. Naturally, socially related examples are the best to use, but any type of anxiety is fine for illustrative purposes.

Once you have gone through a detailed example of how fear reduces with exposure, you are in a position to point out some of the basic principles of exposure using some concrete examples.

Basic Principles of Exposure

Repetition

Clients need to realize that simply doing something once will not reduce their fear completely. Exposure needs to be performed repeatedly in order to completely convince a person that the threat they expected in the situation is actually very unlikely to occur. Often, when clients have an initial success with an exposure exercise, they are reluctant to repeat it. They may say that it is not necessary because they can now do it. However, it is more likely that they are worried that the success was a single lucky instance. It is very important to ensure that they do the exercise again, several times. If they are really not anxious, then it won't matter anyway, but successful exposure generally requires repeated demonstrations of success.

Research into the issue of repetition is confusing. There is a question in the research literature about whether it is more effective to mass practice (i.e., repeat practices very rapidly in succession) or to space practice (i.e., spread practices apart over time). In fact, empirical evidence is equivocal (Chambless 1990). It is important that practices are not too far apart so that clients don't forget about their previous experience between times but it probably doesn't matter how close together the practices are, just as long as they are done repeatedly. In most instances, the frequency of practice will be determined by practical considerations. As a rule, we often suggest that clients do several practices per week (three major items is a good number). These may not all be of the same situation because of practical restrictions, such as expense, limited access, or difficulty of organization. However, if practical considerations allow, having your client practice the same situation at least three times in a week (i.e. every other day), is a good target to aim for.

Duration of Practice

This is one of the most confusing issues for therapists. Once a client enters a feared situation, should she leave immediately, or stay for one minute, one hour, one day? Clearly, leaving immediately constitutes escape and is more likely to worsen the problem rather than improve it. Beyond this, however, the answers are not clear. Ideally, it would be best for the client to stay for extremely long periods. This is the best way for her to really learn that nothing bad is going to happen and that she can tolerate the anxiety, which will eventually pass. Even so, repetition is necessary because it is still possible to believe that "nothing bad happened *this time*, but it might next time." Unfortunately, most situations will not allow an individual to stay for extremely long periods because of the nature of the situation, a point to which we will return later.

The traditional rule of thumb among therapists has been to encourage a client to stay in a situation until her anxiety peaks and begins to decline. As mentioned above, ideally, it would be good to allow as much decline as possible. But theoretically, as long as the anxiety has begun to decline, one should get extinction of the fear rather than sensitization. This is the theory! Unfortunately, a very neat study by Jack Rachman and colleagues (1986) raised many questions about this theory. The researchers had two groups of agoraphobics enter feared situations. The subjects rated their fear at various time points on a 0–100 scale. One group (labeled "no escape") was instructed to leave the situation only when their fear had dropped to half its peak level (it was clearly on its way down). The other group ("escape") was told to leave the situation as soon as their fear had reached 70 (very high and possibly still rising). Contrary to theory, both groups improved and there was no difference between them.

Probably a more important problem with the "rule of thumb" theory is one of pure practicalities. Most real life situations do not simply exist passively so that a person can expose herself to them for as long as she pleases. Real life situations come and go, they constantly change, so that doing exposure often becomes a matter of opportunity rather than design. This is especially the case with social situations. For example, imagine that a person fears speaking up in groups. An exposure exercise might involve sitting in a meeting and saying something. Presumably, saying something in a meeting might last for five seconds or as much as sixty seconds, but it cannot continue for hours simply to suit the person's anxiety levels. Therefore, the clinician's rule of thumb goes out the window in the vast majority of social situations.

Does this matter? Luckily, it seems not. Exposure is still an extremely valuable tool in the reduction of social anxiety. So how does this work? We tend to think of exposure as simply acting as a more direct form of cognitive restructuring. In other words, the principle of exposure to a feared event is to help the individual to change her attitudes or beliefs surrounding that event. The necessary duration required to change those beliefs will vary tremendously depending on the situation and the type of belief. For example, a belief such as "I will say something stupid" doesn't imply any time frame and saying something for one second is likely to be almost as educational as saying something for an hour.

So the decision regarding the optimum duration for an exposure exercise is often made on the basis of practicalities. We usually suggest to our clients that they stay in a situation or with an event for as long as they can, within reasonable limits. However, where a particular event only allows for a very brief exposure, this is still OK, as long as this exposure helps to disconfirm an unrealistic belief. In such cases, frequent repetition is especially useful.

Graduated Exposure

Another empirical question relates to the degree of anxiety that is optimal for an individual during exposure. The original method of systematic desensitization designed by Joseph Wolpe (1958) required the subject to relax at all times and in this way to experience the feared event without any actual fear. In contrast, the technique of flooding requires the subject to experience her most feared event in its entirety and thus generate maximal fear. In between, is graduated exposure, a technique that requires exposure to increasingly feared events, thereby allowing for moderate levels of fear. By and large, studies that have compared these techniques have not found a great deal of difference related to the degree of experienced anxiety (the issue of imaginal vs in vivo exposure is a different one) (Gelder et al. 1973). Therefore, once again, we follow the lines of practicality. Going too gradually will produce slow, painstaking gains. This is motivationally bad for both client and therapist. On the other hand, trying to go too fast will result in other motivational problems and you may well lose your client. Therefore, a moderate rate is probably best, and you should leave the actual decision up to your client. In some cases, clients may be extemely avoidant and may require a push to get them going. Occasionally, they may try to take on too much and may experience a "failure." However, in most cases, clients themselves will be able to determine the fastest rate at which they still feel that they can manage. Typically, situations that clients believe they can encounter if necessary, but would prefer to avoid, are a good starting point.

Finally, you will often find that, as with most other aspects of exposure, the rate at which you proceed will be largely determined by availability. For example, a client may have a hierarchy in which she rates meeting a new member of the opposite sex as a moderately difficult item with several easier items on the list. However, imagine that a new colleague arrives at your client's workplace and happens to be of the opposite sex. This may be considered too good an opportunity to miss and you may suggest to your client that she meet this new colleague, even though it is not the next item in the hierarchy. The nature of feared situations for people with social phobia is such that opportunities must often be taken when they arise rather than waiting for the perfect moment.

Subtle Avoidance

Often one of the most difficult aspects to deal with in conducting exposure therapy is what we call *subtle avoidance*. People with social phobia will often engage in very subtle forms of avoidance, making a situation easier to cope with. For example, they may avoid eye contact while speaking with people, or they may go to a party but sit at the edge of the room and approach no one, or they may speak up in a meeting but only after a long silence when they know that no one else wants to speak, and so on. The variety of subtle forms of avoidance is as infinite as the number of people with social phobia. There may be some commonalities, but in general these types of avoidance are idiosyncratic.

Subtle avoidance can create a problem in that your client may well appear to engage in exposure to her feared events but may derive limited benefit because she is still avoiding the most feared aspects of the experience. If this avoidance is very subtle and idiosyncratic, you as the therapist, may not think to change it, and even the client herself may not realize what she is doing. Therefore, it is extremely important to specify in detail the demands of an exposure exercise (e.g., go to a party and make eye contact with three people at some point).

In most cases, subtle avoidance is not a major issue. As long as the client is honest and open about the parameters that produce greater or lesser anxiety, exposure should proceed smoothly. However, if exposure practice seems to stall, and repeated exposure does not seem to produce total comfort in a situation, you may need to consider whether the client is actually exposing herself to everything that is threatening in that situation. It is a good idea to remind clients of the dangers of subtle avoidance. They should be instructed to try to perform those behaviors that are most threatening in a given situation. Teaching your client to ask herself, "What would make this situation harder for me?" is a good skill to learn. If your client identifies ways of approaching a situation that are more difficult, she doesn't necessarily need to do them right then (if they are too hard) but she should make a note of them so that they can be included in the fear hierarchy. In addition, you will need to ask your client about her experiences in great detail so that you can identify any possible sources of subtle avoidance.

Distraction

A closely related topic is the issue of distraction. When they enter a feared situation, some clients will find that they can cope with their fear by distracting themselves from what is going on. Along similar lines, some therapists actually instruct their clients to use distraction as a coping technique during exposure. Whether this is a valuable or harmful practice is difficult to say. In theory, distraction is likely to interfere dramatically with the effects of exposure. Remember our view that exposure works by teaching the individual that what she is afraid of is very unlikely to happen. If a person is able to distract, so that she is "not there" in an emotional sense, then this learning will not occur. Having said this, we need to acknowledge that empirical studies have not actually shown distraction to be detrimental (Craske et al. 1989). However, this is most likely because most people are not very good at distracting themselves, especially when faced with threat. Our suggestion would be that while it is unclear if it has a negative effect, it is probably best to ensure that your client does not distract herself when engaging in exposure. In addition, distraction is likely to interfere with the person's ability to interact effectively in the situation. For example, if the client is busy distracting herself, she may not hear important details in a meeting. It is far better to encourage your client to concentrate on the situation, identify her initial prediction, and determine the realistic evidence for that prediction.

Developing a Hierarchy

Once your client understands the basic concepts of exposure, it is necessary to develop an exposure hierarchy to help guide progress over the coming weeks. The hierarchy is simply a list of feared situations and activities organized in order of difficulty. You may encourage your client to come up with a set of items by herself as a homework exercise. Or you may wish to devote part of a therapy session to this task.

The instructions to the client are simply to brainstorm all the situations, events, and activities she fears and/or avoids. You will probably also wish to add some items that you have identified through your knowledge of the client. You can review the self-report data collected at the beginning of therapy to help guide you. At first, the task is simply to brainstorm items in order to come up with as many as possible. They do not need to be organized or structured in any way.

Next, you will need to decide which of these items is usable. To be included in the hierarchy, items need to be practical and specific. An item such as "meeting the president of the United States" may well be anxiety-provoking for a social phobic, but it is hardly practical. Clients need to be reminded that they are going to have to try to carry out these items. On the other hand, clients should be encouraged not to avoid items that may be difficult to arrange. For example, a person with public speaking anxiety may have difficulty arranging a speaking engagement, but attempts will need to be made to find a relevant situation, such as joining a public speaking group, even though it requires considerable effort. In addition, items need to be clearly described and detailed. An item such as "meet new people" is too vague to be used in the hierarchy. Nevertheless, such vague items should not be discouraged at the brainstorming point because they, in turn, can generate several more detailed items. For example, "meet new people" can be used as a general topic to produce the items "meet a younger person of the same sex," "meet a younger person of the opposite sex," "meet an older person of the same sex," "meet an older person of the opposite sex," and so on. Remember that these items will be used to set homework tasks for your client, so the more detail the better (e.g., initiate a conversation with the receptionist where you work on Tuesday morning).

Once a list of items has been generated, the final task involves having your client order these from the easiest item to the hardest (see John's example, p. 113). Your client may find it useful to assign a number (0–8) to each item to indicate the degree of anxiety likely to be experienced in each. It is very important to tell your client not to worry about the higher items at this stage—they will become easier as she develops more confidence with the lower items. The final list of items may number anywhere between three and three hundred. There is no set number, but the more you have, the more there is to work with. The exposure stage is usually where the client finally gets to see the most tangible change. Therefore, having a very small hierarchy provides limited opportunities for improvement. If you have many items in the hierarchy, you might wish to organize it into several smaller, logically distinguished hierarchies, such as initiating conversations, public speaking, or attending social events. There are no rules. We are simply talking about a logical way to organize your client's homework exercises.

Finally, you will need to make sure that there are no gaps that appear too large. Having items that are closer in anxiety ratings will better facilitate generalization, as coping skills will be more easily transferred from one situation to another. Adjoining items on the hierarchy should be no more than one or at most two points apart on the 0–8 scale of anxiety. If your client has generated a hierarchy with large gaps showing several very easy items and several very difficult items, you will need to try to encourage her to generate a few in between. Often this can be done by modifying one of the other items. For example, an item such as "going to a party where I don't know anyone" could be made easier by including a previous item, "going with one friend to a party where I don't know anyone."

Conducting Exposure

Conducting exposure is quite simply a matter of getting your client to begin to do the activities set out in the hierarchy. Obviously, she would begin with the lower items and move on to gradually higher and higher items as anxiety to the lower ones reduces. As confidence builds, anxiety to the more difficult items will reduce. As we discussed earlier, it is often not possible to move up the hierarchy in a totally structured order due to practical constraints. Therefore, the client should tackle the lowest items that are available. However, you should try to ensure that any items your client does attempt are neither too easy nor too difficult. As a rough rule, we generally suggest that items with an anxiety rating of around 3–5 are good to attempt. Any lower, and little learning will occur. Any higher, and the client is more likely to have a negative experience.

An important point to remember is that clients do not have to wait for exposure situations to occur naturally. Many exposure tasks can actually be forced with the explicit intention of providing practice. For example, the opportunity for an item such as "having a drink in front of a group of people" may take a long time to arise naturally. However, it is very easy to go to a bar or coffee shop intentionally and have drinks in front of lots of people, purely for the sake of the practice this provides. By forcing the situation in this way, a client can do simple tasks like this many times per week. Some clients will argue that they do not normally do those activities and will never want to. But it should be emphasized to them that the purpose at this point is to provide opportunities for practice, not simply to do practical tasks.

There are several ways of conducting exposure and several issues that therapists need to consider. We will discuss these here.

Imaginal vs in Vivo Exposure

There has been an ongoing debate about whether exposure is better when conducted imaginally or *in vivo* (live). Empirical evidence seems to indicate that in vivo exposure produces faster and more extensive results (Emmelkamp & Wessels 1975). The exception might be for clients who are especially good at imagery. However, for most, direct experience seems to be the way to go.

Having said this, we recommend two circumstances under which you should conduct imaginal exposure as a first step prior to in vivo. Imaginal exposure is particularly useful as a first step for those clients who are highly avoidant or extremely anxious. In addition to provoking anxiety in a more controllable way (controlled by the therapist), imaginal exposure allows clients to practice their coping strategies in the safety of your office. Imaginal exposure alone may also be necessary for certain cases where it is just not possible to conduct in vivo exposure. For example, your client may report anxiety over going to parties but she may not yet have the friends with whom to be invited to parties. In this case, you could expose your client to the situation imaginally. This can be conducted several times so that if the opportunity to attend a party finally arises, your client will be ready and not let the opportunity go by. In most cases it is also possible to simulate impractical situations (such as the above) and thereby enhance the effects of the imaginal exposure. For example, you may encourage your client to go to bars, clubs, and so on, in an effort to approximate the party situation.

We also want to note that some therapists like to conduct imaginal exposure for each item on the hierarchy. Thus, a highly comprehensive format is followed for each feared situation in which the client cognitively restructures her thoughts relating to the situation, does imaginal exposure to the situation with the therapist, and engages in *in vivo* exposure to the situation. If this type of structured format is preferable for you, we would certainly support it. However, our position is that it may not be necessary in all cases, as many of the successful empirically validated programs do not include an imaginal exposure component.

Coping Strategies

There is also considerable debate over the need to include coping strategies for clients. Wolpe's original desensitization procedure was based on detailed training in relaxation before exposure began. Since that time, empirical evidence has clearly indicated that the active ingredient in any package is exposure to the feared situation (Barlow 1988). Inclusion of various coping strategies seems to make little difference. Therefore, we do not recommend the use of any additional coping strategies (such as relaxation, meditation, etc.) during exposure.

It should be noted that we do not include the cognitive restructuring exercise in this category. As discussed, we view exposure as an extension of cognitive restructuring—that is, a way of gathering direct evidence. Encouraging clients to use cognitive restructuring while encountering the feared situation is a very useful way of reinforcing this message and helping to produce a new belief.

Finally, a word about the use of medication may be useful. Empirical evidence does not seem to support the suggestion that medication can enhance the effects of exposure (Chambless et al. 1982). In fact, theoretically, there may be reason to expect that medication may detract from exposure under certain circumstances, making the exercise less effective. Remember that we argue that exposure produces its effects by helping to form new beliefs. It is very important that the client learns that, "When I am in this situation, what I am afraid of is very unlikely to occur." If a client takes medication each time she exposes herself to a feared event, she risks developing the attitude "When I am in this situation, what I am afraid of is very unlikely to occur *as long as I take this pill*." In this case, any time the client does not take the pill, fear may well return, as the client attributes her success only to the presence of the pill. In addition, the client never actually learns to tolerate the anxious arousal, an important step in exposure therapy.

Many of your clients will be on medication. Treatment can still be conducted and, in most cases, this will have little consequence. However, it is important to discuss these types of attitudes with your client and keep an eye out for her failure to attribute her success to her own ability. To facilitate this, it is important to schedule non-medicated exposures into the hierarchy and, when possible, repeat some of the exposures after your client has ceased medication.*

---

*Note: It is always advisable that changes in medication be done in consultation with a medical practitioner.

Therapist Accompaniment

Finally, it will be necessary for you to decide whether you will accompany your client on exposure outings. The few studies that have addressed this issue have failed to find evidence that therapist-accompanied exposure provides any advantage over unaccompanied exposure (Ghosh and Marks 1987). However, there is no doubt that many clients will have some difficulties with exposure, especially in the early stages. Accompanying a client can get the ball rolling by providing them with guidance and reassurance during the exercise. It may also be of some benefit at first to have someone there to prompt the client to engage in cognitive restructuring and generate more realistic appraisals of the evidence. However, if you decide to accompany your client on some initial exposures, we recommend that this be limited to only a few situations so that the client can reduce any dependence on you.

There may be some situations in which the client is unwilling to expose herself at first without a companion, such as going to a coffee shop and sitting at the counter. If you are unwilling to attend such events, it is often useful to include a significant other into exposure. With the client's permission it may be of value to ask the significant other to attend one or two of the therapy sessions. In this way, this person can also learn the principles of the techniques and can act as an "honorary therapist" *in vivo*. In such instances, the significant other can assist the client in cognitive restructuring during the exercises. In addition, including a significant other is also a useful tactic in the case of difficult or disorganized clients, because it provides additional accountability to those who tend not to do their homework.

John B.'s Example

Because of John's extensive avoidance behavior, it was easy for him to generate a large number of feared situations. Following brainstorming by John, he and the therapist together tried to organize the items into logically related categories. Five hierarchies were identified: work, friendships, romantic relationships, general interaction, and general observation. For example, the work hierarchy contained situations related to fears and avoidance behavior at work, from minor habits at one end to his fears about getting a promotion at the other. The general interaction hierarchy contained various miscellaneous items related to John's fears of interacting with other people such as talking to shop assistants, asking for favors, and asking for information. Similarly, the general observation hierarchy contained items related to John's fears of being observed by others, such as walking in busy areas, getting on crowded buses, wearing outlandish clothes, and going out with his hair uncombed.

Once the brainstormed items had been divided into the five areas, it was noticed that one or two areas lacked breadth of coverage. For example, the romance hierarchy actually contained only one item, going on a blind date, which was rated at the maximum level of fear, 8. The therapist helped John to generate a few more items to cover lower levels of anxiety. For example, for the romance hierarchy, the therapist suggested some low-level items (e.g., saying hello to several single women at work, calling a singles telephone line to practice talking to women) and some medium level items (e.g., going to a local community dance, asking one of the women from work to coffee).

For homework, an attempt was made each week to select items from several of the hierarchies. Given John's recent tendency to turn to alcohol to help him get through situations, particular attention was paid by the therapist to reminding John that alcohol should not be used. If John felt a strong need to drink in a situation, then it was presumably too high up the hierarchy and he needed to practice something lower. When situations involved alcohol, such as interacting in a bar, John was encouraged not to drink, not because the aim of therapy was to promote abstinence, but because, as an exposure exercise, it was important that John be able to interact without the use of alcohol.

As a more detailed example, John's friendship hierarchy is shown in Table 8–1.

Homework

Homework for this session is quite simply to begin conducting exposure. Discuss with your client which items from the hierarchy she is going to do and exactly when, where, and how she will organize herself to do them. Writing down the prescribed exposure exercises is a good way to increase the client's compliance. The number of items will obviously vary depending on many factors, such as your

Table 8–1. Sample exposure hierarchy for John—friendship situations.

Friendship Stepladder	Expected Anxiety (0–8)
Organizing a barbecue for several people	8
Joining work colleagues in bar after work (no alcohol)	7
Joining social groups (e.g., art class, dance class)	7
Joining the main lunch group at work	5+
Inviting a neighbor over for barbecue	5
Making a substantive comment to female colleague	4
Engaging a male colleague in longer conversation	3–4
Making a neutral comment to a female colleague	2
Making a more substantive comment (e.g., about football) to a male colleague	2
Making a neutral comment (e.g., about the weather) to a male colleague	1

client's motivation, the size and ease of the items, practicality, and so on. You can certainly allow an easing in period in the first week, but you should not allow your client to do too little. You will often find that clients will be hesitant to begin with and fears will decrease their motivation, but when gains become noticeable, motivation will increase dramatically. Therefore, some pushing on your part may be necessary to get the ball rolling.

As usual, it is a good idea for clients to monitor their progress. We have included a sample monitoring form (see Table 8–2). This will help clients chart their improvements and will help you in case of any difficulties.

Dealing with Difficulties

Lack of Motivation

In vivo exposure is inherently an unpleasant technique. Imagine how you might feel walking naked through the middle of Main Street and you might get an idea of the level of anxiety your client will experience. The basic rule, "you have to become anxious to overcome anxiety" is a good motto to convey to clients. An empathic but firm approach is necessary. Specifically, you need to empathize with the client's difficulty and the anxiety provoked by social situations, yet at the same time stress that exposure is the only effective way to reduce excessive fears and is therefore a necessary part of treatment.

Given the rigors of exposure, it is no wonder that motivation may lag for many clients. As we discussed earlier, all clients will have some difficulty motivating themselves. But for most, the gains they notice will make up for any unpleasantness. Reminding clients of the rationale for exposure can help at times when motivation flags.

Some clients will have particular problems carrying out the exposure exercises. Very often it is the more severe cases who are very highly anxious or very avoidant. There is often an underlying belief such as "I must never get anxious," or "I will break if I get anxious,"

Table 8–2. Form for recording exposure practice.

Situation/Event	Date/Time	Duration	Expected Anxiety (0–8)	Actual Anxiety (0–8)	Comments (e.g., unforeseen occurrences, subtle avoidance, coping strategies, etc.)

which can be challenged. In some cases, you may also need to proceed very slowly, breaking the steps into very small ones and moving very gradually up the hierarchy. However, if progress becomes so slow as to be undetectable, you may need to push the client along or else discuss with her the concept that she may never change. It may also be of value to set very specific exercises. Determine the exact date and time at which the client will conduct her exposure and have her call you immediately after to report on how it went. If you have the time and resources to accompany a client on an exposure exercise, this may be the case in which it is particularly warranted. Ultimately, of course, it is the client's decision. In the rare case where a client will not do exposure, you may simply have to explain that her anxiety is very unlikely to change. You may want to proceed with cognitive restructuring alone at this point, and hope that you will make enough inroads to facilitate initiation of exposure at a later time.

Lack of Effectiveness

In most cases, as long as exposure is carried out, gains will be noticed. However, there may be times when exposure is being conducted but anxiety does not reduce. In these cases, you need to check exactly what has occurred. Have your client describe her exposure, moment by moment, and determine where things went wrong. We have already discussed several ways in which the underlying irrational belief can be protected from the corrective benefits of exposure, such as via subtle avoidance, distraction, or medication. These factors need to be evaluated. In addition, prior to each exposure exercise, it is very useful to actually go through cognitive restructuring with respect to the forthcoming exposure situation. Have your client try to identify her initial belief, examine the evidence, identify the consequence, and so on. This should be done on the usual cognitive restructuring form and a copy of it carried to the next exposure session. The client can then use this sheet to remind herself of the restructured beliefs before and during the exposure. This will facilitate her ability to generate rational thoughts during the exposure exercise and will aid more permanent attitude change.

Sometimes you might find that exposure is not challenging the correct belief. If you recall, cognitive restructuring identifies a series of beliefs, each at a so-called lower level. In some cases, exposure is able to challenge the surface level, but not the more underlying beliefs. For example, a client may be anxious about public speaking. The initial belief might be "I will forget my lines," and the consequence may be "people will think I'm stupid." The client might give several speeches, but in doing so work extremely hard each night to learn all her lines (working obsessively in this way can be considered a type of subtle avoidance). When the client then gives speeches, she is learning that she will not forget her lines (surface belief), but she is not learning that *if* she forgets her lines, most people are still not very likely to think she is stupid (underlying belief). Exposure needs to be modified to allow testing of this second-level belief. For example, the client can be instructed to give a speech with minimal preparation or may even be told to intentionally get some of her lines wrong, to have a long pause in the middle, and so on. She might then try to get feedback from members of the audience to check what they thought.

Dealing with "Failures"

Sometimes clients will return to the next session looking sheepish and saying that they could not do what they set out to do. At other times, they may come in with tears in their eyes saying what a disaster the experience had been.

The first point to make to your client is that there is no actual failure with in vivo exposure. Step one is to reinforce the client for actually doing the exercise. Judge success in the beginning by whether she did the exercise, not how she felt. You will expect her to feel anxious. In fact, anxiety may well increase at first because your client may now be confronting situations she has avoided for years. Fear will eventually subside with repetitive exposures. In addition, even if the exercise went badly, you should take a problem-solving approach. For example, "great—this is a chance to look at what you were thinking that caused the anxiety," rather than seeing it as a failure. A lesson can be learned from each experience, good or bad. You need to discuss the incident with the client and identify together all of the things that she could learn from the experience, what went well and what went wrong.

Next, you should go back over the experience and help the client apply her cognitive restructuring to the supposed failure. The main points are that not doing everything she set out to do is not the end of the world; she can simply try again, and so on. It is very important for the client to view the so-called failure as a temporary hitch rather than becoming totally demoralized. In fact, you may even suggest to her that you expect things to be difficult, especially in the beginning. That way, she will be less likely to develop unrealistic expectations about progress and not become demoralized when things do not proceed so smoothly.

Finally, you need to encourage another attempt, hopefully as soon as possible. Discuss with the client why she feels she couldn't go through with the task. In some cases there might be extenuating circumstances. She may have been feeling more anxious than usual that day. In this case, the same exercise can be set. On the other hand, you and your client might decide that the exercise was somewhat harder for her than expected. Part of the exposure plan is to collect data, so if this is what you found, you will need to revise the treatment plan accordingly. In this case, it is a good idea to break the exercise down into smaller, less anxiety-provoking steps. For example, you might get a significant other to accompany the client the first time, or the client might select a time when there are fewer people present. It is a good idea to teach this principle to your client in general. That is, if an exposure attempt suddenly turns out to be too difficult, the client should look for ways to make it a little easier, and then go through with it. For example, imagine that one exposure involved asking a question in a large lecture. When the time came, the client may have suddenly realized that this was too hard a task and may not have been able to do it. She should then have tried something a little easier, such as going up to the speaker after the talk and asking an individual question. In this way, the exercise was not completely a failure and something valuable was achieved.

Finally, it is important with all clients to point out that exposure is not a smooth process. There are always ups and downs. Just because a client was able to perform one task on one particular day does not mean she will necessarily be able to do that same task the next day. Performance in exposure tasks will fluctuate with a person's general mood and confidence, things that vary a great deal depending on many factors in a person's life. As described earlier, clients should be taught that if they feel they cannot perform a task one day, they need to try a slightly easier task and then go back to the harder task when they are feeling more confident. Usually, clients will have had the problem for a long time and breaking the pattern will take considerable effort. Providing clients with realistic expectations will decrease their frustration and negative reactions to the process and will set the stage for effective therapy.

9

Feedback and Social Skills

AIMS

1. Assessing deficits (perceived or real).
2. Providing realistic feedback of performance.
3. Teaching skills where needed and increasing confidence.

BACKGROUND

Many situations feared by people with social phobia involve some degree of competent social performance. These might include meeting new people, presenting reports, going on a first date, or asking someone a favor. In such situations, the evaluation a person receives is, to some extent, under his control. That is, the better his performance, the more positive the evaluation from the other party. In addition, given that people monitor their own performance, the better the performance, the less anxiety experienced. Therefore, teaching your client good skills and abilities will help to reduce his anxiety.

Having said this, there is a very important caveat to discuss. Confidence, or conversely anxiety, from a given performance arises from an individual's *perception* of how he is performing. Perceptions may be more or less accurate. As we have emphasized, the cognitive styles of people with social phobia are biased toward the negative. Thus, you should not be surprised to learn that this is exactly the same with perceptions of social performance.

Studies (e.g., Rapee and Lim 1992) have demonstrated that people with social phobia tend to underestimate their social performance relative to judgments made by independent raters. That is, when asked to evaluate their own performance in a social situation, people with social phobia score it considerably lower than observers do. Further, the degree of this discrepancy is much greater than it is for people without social phobia. What this means for your client is that he may well feel anxious in a situation because he *believes* he is performing poorly, even when, in fact, he is not. For example, when meeting a new person, your client may feel as though he said several stupid things and came across very badly, but in fact, the other person may well have felt that he was very pleasant. In this case, simply providing realistic feedback may be enough to shift this belief. On the other hand, teaching social skills may still be valuable because it may be the most powerful way to help the client believe that he is now performing much better, even though in reality there may not have been much need for change.

Assessment of Social Performance

Naturally, the first step is to assess the performance of your client to determine whether skills are actually as poor as he believes, and to identify exactly which skills require work and in what ways.

The most practical method for assessing social performance is the use of role play. You may ask a colleague or significant other to interact with your client while you observe, or you might act in the role play yourself. In most cases your client will be able to identify one or two specific situations of particular concern. You would simply set up such a situation as realistically as possible and act it out. It is a good idea to try to go at least ten to fifteen minutes in order to allow the client to really immerse himself in the role. It is also extremely valuable to video the entire interaction if possible. This will provide a useful method for later feedback and training and will also allow you time to view the performance at leisure.

When the client performs the role play, it will be necessary for you to gauge his perception of the performance. This can be done qualitatively by simply discussing your client's beliefs and feelings as part of debriefing. However, it is also useful to provide a quantitative evaluation of the performance that can be repeated at various times. To design a quantitative measure, you need to list several criteria for good performance on the specific task and then simply provide a scale on which the client can rate each criterion. You may want to provide both global criteria (e.g., "generally friendly") as well as specific criteria (e.g., "smiled appropriately"). It is a good idea for you to rate your view of the performance using the same form for later feedback purposes. A sample measure from our study of public speaking performance is provided in Table 9–1.

Aside from set role play, you might also be able to assess your client's social performance by direct observation. Obviously the range of situations will be limited, but there are many that you can observe. Public performances such as speeches, acting, or recitals are obvious candidates. But there may be other situations that you can set up, for example, asking your client to try engaging your secretary in conversation. If you accompany your client on any exposure exercises, these will also provide opportunities to observe skills. As with the role play, it will be necessary to debrief after the exercise and obtain your client's views of his performance. Again, quantitative ratings of the performance by both you and your client will be valuable for feedback and comparative purposes.

Table 9–1. Measure of public speaking performance.

Please rate your performance on the speech you just gave using the items listed below. For each item indicate on the scale how you thought you came across to the audience.

	not at all	slightly	moder- ately	much	very much
Content was understandable					
Kept eye contact with audience					
Stuttered					
Had long pauses					
Fidgeted					
"Um"ed and "Ah"ed					
Had a clear voice					
Seemed to tremble and shake					
Sweated					
Blushed					
Face twitched					
Voice quivered					
Appeared confident					
Appeared nervous					
Kept audience interested					
Generally spoke well					
Made a good impression					

Providing Feedback

Provision of feedback about your client's performance will follow directly from the assessment. Feedback should be reassuring and/ or constructive. By reassuring, we mean feedback designed to inform the client that his performance was better than he thinks and to highlight its good features. By constructive feedback, we mean feedback designed to point out ways of improving the client's performance. We will discuss this latter type of feedback in the next section.

According to the model of social phobia presented earlier, lack of social skills is not a necessary factor in social phobia. Most of your clients will have adequate skills for most situations, although they may not always use them. As discussed earlier, the most likely scenario is that your client will falsely believe that his skills are inadequate. Your task is to provide evidence to the contrary.

Naturally, the most obvious method is for you to provide verbal feedback, based on your observations. Specific, detailed feedback is likely to be much more valuable than broad, nonspecific feedback. Going over your quantitative scoring of the performance and comparing this with your client's scoring will also be more believable.

Unfortunately, simple feedback from the therapist is often not especially believable. Clients are easily able to discount it by saying that it is your job to try to be nice, or that you are more understanding because you are a therapist. Therefore, any support you can get from others will be of value. In a group situation, the other members of the group should provide feedback. Otherwise, with the client's permission, you may try to involve a colleague or other outsider in the observation and feedback.

Probably the most valuable source of feedback is the use of a video. It is very important that you instruct your client to try to view the video in an impartial manner. Most of us feel self-conscious and anxious when viewing our own performance for the first time and this can often lead us to perceive it in a negative fashion. However, by intentionally trying to view our performance as if we were viewing a stranger, it is possible to override this tendency. In a recent study we were able to show that people with social phobia are able to take an objective position with respect to video recordings of their own performance when they are instructed to do so (Rapee and Hayman 1996). Further, in this study, subjects who viewed their performance from video had a more realistic appraisal of a subsequent performance, even when video was not used. You can use the video recording of the performance to support your verbal feedback and to point out that others cannot see most of what goes on inside the individual.

Finally, some of the most powerful realistic feedback can be obtained during in vivo exercises, most easily in combination with exposure. In many cases, it will not be possible to obtain performance feedback in this way, but, with a little ingenuity, there are many situations in which it can be done. Prior to exposure exercises, you and your client should try to brainstorm ways in which feedback can be obtained. For example, your client may try to eavesdrop on people who might be discussing his performance. Or he may simply ask someone for an honest appraisal. Alternately, he may simply look at the end result, such as whether the customer buys the product, or whether the other person agrees to another date. Of course, it may also be a good idea to go through some cognitive restructuring practice to remind your client how to deal with "bad" news. For example, assuming the performance wasn't adequate, what is the realistic consequence of that?

By putting together a collection of different sources of feedback across various situations, your client should begin to learn that his social performance is actually better than he thinks. This will help to build confidence and reduce the fear that he will be negatively evaluated. But what happens if your assessment indicates that there are aspects of the performance that could use some work? In this case your honest feedback will need to point out these limitations and you will need to help your client develop the necessary skills.

Improving Social Performance

Despite the fact that people with social phobia will not necessarily have deficits in social skills, you may come across the individual client who does indeed lack appropriate behaviors. In addition, most people can benefit from training in good social performance, both to fine tune skills and to provide a feeling of mastery.

For many clients, simple provision of information will be suffi-cient to improve their social performance. Many social situations such as giving speeches, dating, or going on job interviews are asso-ciated with specific skills and abilities on which many of us could improve. There are many practical books that go into these behav-iors in detail. Going through these particular skills with your client and discussing them in the context of your feedback from the assess-ment will be most beneficial.

The model of social phobia that we are using hypothesizes that a major factor in social phobia is an *apparent* lack of social skills due to subtle avoidance. That is, these people may well possess the skills but may not use them in the appropriate situations because they are avoiding the possibility of negative evaluation. That is to say, the observed deficit is caused by the anxiety, which is inhibiting appro-priate behavior, and not an inability to perform a specific skill. For example, an individual may have an opinion on a topic being dis-cussed by a group of people but may remain silent, not because he doesn't know what to say, but because he doesn't want to call atten-tion to himself or have others evaluate his opinion. This is a situa-tion where feedback is especially needed. The feedback needs to point out to the client the sorts of avoidance behaviors he is engag-ing in and also the fact that he knows what to do but is holding back due to anxiety. In fact, this type of subtle avoidance may not always be apparent in assessments that are conducted within therapy ses-sions, because if the client is comfortable with the therapist, he may well perform adequately. You may need to specifically inquire about these situations and ask the client what he normally does in real-life situations. If avoidance appears to be a problem, the client needs to be made aware of it and these behaviors can then be specifically targeted during exposure.

Your client can also improve his social performance by observing others in social situations, especially those who are very proficient. You should encourage your client to identify people in various social situations whom he admires and believes are particularly socially adept. He should then watch what these people do and how they act. Again, it will be important for your client to be very specific in these observations. He should identify specific behaviors that appear to achieve the most positive effects and then compare them to his own repertoire. In other words, rather than simply saying, "I could never be that good," your client needs to ask himself, "What *particular* things is X doing that I don't do?" Then, the next time he does some exposure, your client should try to include one or two of these behaviors.

Finally, the most effective way of teaching social skills, especially where there are clear deficits, is via role play with extensive feedback. Given the nature of social phobia, it is important not to appear as though you are criticizing your client. Instead, it is best to explain that as a result of having social anxiety, he has avoided situations and has not fully developed his skills, not because of a personal deficiency, but due to a lack of practice. At this stage the use of a video is invaluable, but in this case it would be used to point out deficiencies in the client's performance and help him understand how they can be overcome. The overall process should be one of gradual shaping. A role play is conducted and feedback is given about the specific behaviors that are problematic as well as suggested ways of performing differently. It is best not to focus on too many behaviors at a time. The role play is then repeated with the client attempting to improve on his performance. This is followed by more feedback, and so on. For a more detailed discussion of training in social skills, the client is referred to a self-help book by David Burns (1985). For an extended discussion of social skills training the therapist should see Hargie et al. (1994) or Trower (1986).

John B.'s Example

There were several areas in which John showed some minor deficiencies. The most obvious of these was in casual verbal interactions with other people, especially females. This was made a central target of feedback and skills training.

To assess John's verbal interaction skills, a role play was set up. With John's permission, a female colleague of the therapist was included and the two were told to pretend that they were at a party. Neither of them knew anyone else. Julie was sitting alone in a corner and John's task was to strike up a conversation with her. The role play continued for ten minutes and was videoed. Overall, John's skills were not bad and there were several positive aspects. When John was asked for his impressions, he looked dejected and said how awful everything had gone. He felt that he had made no positive impression on Julie at all.

The therapist then showed John the video of the performance and provided his own feedback as it progressed. On the first feedback occasion, the therapist focused on several positive aspects of the interaction that John had seemed to ignore. These included his pleasant smile, his detection of Julie's interest in skiing, and his gentle manner. In addition, the overall feel of the role play was not especially different from a performance one might expect to see from anyone else. Via the video feedback, John was able to appreciate that his performance had not been as bad as he had first thought. In addition, he was able to appreciate several of his own positive attributes. The therapist also asked Julie to provide some feedback to John about how she felt he had come across. Her main point was that she didn't feel he had appeared very nervous and she also reinforced some of the positive aspects that had been pointed out by the therapist. These sources of feedback were very important to John who began to realize that how he *feels* he comes across is not necessarily how he appears to the outside world.

Next, the therapist pointed out to John that while the performance had not been bad, there were several aspects that could be improved. The video was replayed and these deficits were reviewed. They included nonoptimal eye contact, a somewhat flat voice tone, and excessively long silences. In addition, John appeared a little stilted and hesitant. He and the therapist then discussed issues having to do with appropriate and inappropriate eye contact, voice tone, and use of silence. John also expressed a concern that he was unsure, when conversing, of what to say next, and as a result spent much of his time thinking about the next topic rather than focusing on the conversation. The therapist asked John to brainstorm various topics that could be covered with just about anyone and also did some brief cognitive restructuring regarding the worst case scenario if conversation did run out. In addition, John was instructed to use his attentional focus when conversing. Rather than focusing his attention on the next possible topic or wondering whether he looked natural, John needed to focus directly on what his partner was saying when she spoke and on what he himself was saying when it was his turn.

The therapist conducted several brief practices and role plays with John to practice each of these components and to provide feedback after each. Finally, Julie was again asked to come in and another ten-minute role play was conducted and videoed. For homework, John was instructed to engage as many different people as possible in conversation.

Homework

Much of the work on social performance will occur in session. Therefore, for homework, the client should continue to practice his in vivo exposure and cognitive restructuring. Any identified subtle avoidance that handicaps performance should be especially targeted. If you have suggested combining exposure with feedback from others, this modification should be given as homework. Similarly, you may give the client an exercise in observing the performance of an adept other.

10

*

Addressing Special Issues

UNASSERTIVENESS

Lack of assertiveness is a common problem among people with so-cial phobia. In fact, it should really be thought of as a component of social phobia and does not need its own section as it is likely to be encountered during cognitive restructuring and exposure exercises. The reason for raising it here is that many popular psychology books have been written addressing this specific issue and many clients present with this specific concern.

The assertiveness situation can simply be conceptualized as an-other social/evaluative situation and, as such, assertiveness train-ing can be easily conceptualized as falling within the standard treat-ment for social phobia. While different terms may be used, the three components most commonly included in assertiveness train-ing packages can be labelled skills training, cognitive restructur-ing, and exposure.

Skills Training

As for most social skills, people with social phobia rarely lack the ability to be assertive. It is much more common for these individuals to simply avoid being assertive, due to beliefs that others will evaluate them negatively if they act assertively, or to catastrophize about others' response to their assertiveness. Therefore, cognitive restructuring and exposure are essential treatment components in most cases. Nevertheless, skills training can still be useful, as many people are not as effective in being assertive as they could be, and people with social phobia are no exception. In addition, practice in the skills of assertiveness can help to increase confidence in one's ability to be assertive. Reviewing skills often helps the client realize that she actually does have them, thereby increasing confidence. Therefore, it is often a good idea to begin with a brief coverage of how to be assertive. Since there are many good books that cover the subject in detail, we will provide only a brief summary here.

Lange and Jakubowski (1976) coined the term *responsible assertiveness* to convey the idea that assertive actions should be carried out with consideration for the other person. They distinguish among three types of behaviors: unassertive, aggressive, and assertive. Clients need to be carefully taught the distinctions among these three.

Unassertive behavior involves acknowledging other people's rights while ignoring one's own. This is the common pattern in social phobia. People with social phobia are usually able to see very clearly all the reasons why the other person has the right to get his/her way, but are not able to apply the same reasoning to their own situation. Aggressive behavior involves acknowledging one's own rights while ignoring the rights of others. Finally, assertive behavior involves a balanced view of expressing one's own rights and desires while still acknowledging the importance of the rights of others. Therefore, as pointed out by Lange and Jacubowsky, assertiveness does not always involve getting one's own way. Rather it involves being able to express one's own needs but at the same time realizing that in certain circumstances, other people's needs may be more important than one's own. Examples of these three types of behaviors are listed in Table 10–1.

In teaching assertiveness to your clients, you may wish to spend some time discussing the issue of personal rights, and, in particular, where the client sees herself fitting into society. At the very least, increasing insight into this issue can help a client to become more contented with where she is. For example, one of us recently saw a client who was very upset about a dog that regularly barked next door. We discussed assertiveness and how she could ask the neighbors politely to try to keep their dog quiet, and if this did not work, it was within her rights to complain to the local council. However, in discussing rights, the client decided that she in fact did not have the right to keep an animal silent, or to have a pet taken away from its owners. Even though the client was unable to be assertive in this

Table 10–1. Examples of assertive, aggressive, and unassertive behavior.

Situation	Unassertive Response	Aggressive Response	Assertive Response
Being asked a favor that is not possible	I guess I can try to fit it in.	You've got to be kidding.	I realize it is important for you, but I'm afraid my time is full up today.
Wanting to ask a favor that is not very pleasant	Avoidance—i.e., don't ask	I want you to do something for me.	It would really help me a great deal if you would be able to do this for me.
Reacting to an inconvenience	I guess I'll just live with it.	Stop that right now!	I would really prefer it if you could move elsewhere to do that.

situation, realizing that it was her choice not to do so dramatically reduced the distress she experienced when the dog barked. It is important to realize as a therapist that you should not force your views onto your client. Each person will have a different view of her rights in various situations, often influenced by religion, culture, or upbringing. Your job is to help your client understand the link between assumed rights and assertive behavior and to help explore her concept of personal rights.

Once you have covered the issue of rights, you then need to ensure that your client understands the power of communication (both verbal and nonverbal) in providing assertive, unassertive, and aggressive messages. You may provide a few hypothetical situations and get your client to generate the different types of responses. Audio or video taping these responses and playing them back to the client is a powerful method of demonstrating how each one comes across. From here, it might be necessary for some clients to discuss different ways in which assertive messages can be best expressed. The pop psychology books on assertiveness will have lots of tricks and examples. Some of the more common principles are:

1. Owning your own feelings—for example, using the word "I" in statements.
2. Expressing to the other person the consequences of his/her behavior on you (e.g., when you do x, I feel y).
3. Providing clear, explicit suggestions for what you wish to achieve (e.g., I would really appreciate it if you could turn your radio down a little).
4. Listening to the other person's points and acknowledging that you have understood them, for example, by reflecting.

Finally, of course, lots of practice via role play is essential. Plenty of feedback during these exercises can help to shape the client's behaviors.

Cognitive Restructuring

Having skills in assertive behavior is not enough. Most people with social phobia are unwilling to use their assertiveness skills because they believe that others will not like them, or will be angry with them if they assert their rights. To some extent they may be correct. It is probably true that if you are very assertive when you first meet someone, his or her initial impression of you will be more negative than if you were less assertive. However, it needs to be pointed out to clients that their friends, family, and even acquaintances know them in an entire context. Expressing one's rights from time to time will do little to change others' overall opinions of you. Of course, if one were to assert oneself all the time, this might be different, but that would be approaching aggression.

The standard cognitive restructuring exercise needs to be applied. Clients should identify their initial belief and then examine the evidence for that belief. The technique of putting oneself in the other's position is a very good one. For example, "How would you feel if someone said that to you?" Examination of consequences is also important. A common consequence is "s/he will be angry with me." When the client thinks about it realistically, she will often realize that this is not such a tragedy. In addition, many people actually prefer others to deal directly and assertively with them.

Exposure

Finally, you should encourage your client to practice assertive behaviors in a standard exposure format. Your client should be able to brainstorm a number of assertiveness situations that differ in degree of difficulty. These can then be placed into their own exposure hierarchy. If situations do not arise naturally, many assertiveness situations can be set up so that practice can be accelerated. For example, one can easily buy products with the intention of returning them, or one can intentionally ask someone a favor, even if it is not especially important.

PROCRASTINATION

You may find some clients who approach you to help them with chronic procrastination. The first step in such a case is to conduct a thorough assessment, particularly focusing on the underlying motivations for the procrastination. As with any problem, a functional analysis should form the basis of your treatment. Procrastination may be a result of obsessional beliefs, general disorganization, difficulties with time management, or simply lack of motivation. These issues cannot be dealt with in this program. However, in many cases, procrastination may be a complication of social anxiety. Delaying chores or work assignments is often a result of perfectionistic concerns which, in turn, can be conceptualized as a type of social fear. For example, a student may not feel able to begin studying and may find a thousand different excuses. Discussion of the situation may indicate that the student holds an unrealistic belief that she must do brilliantly on the exam or she is a failure. She may further believe that a brilliant score is not possible and, therefore, may delay studying, due to the anxiety this belief raises.

Theoretically, the issue of self-handicapping (Snyder and Smith 1982) is an important one here. According to self-handicapping theory, individuals may fail to perform adaptive behaviors in order to protect their self-esteem. For example, the student taking the exam may intentionally not study because to study and fail would mean that she was stupid. If she did not study and failed the exam, she would be able to believe that the failure was due to the lack of studying, hence preserving self-esteem. People with social phobia commonly engage in self-handicapping, for example, not giving their all in various situations. As a result, they often do not do as well as they could if they put more effort into things.

Clearly, treatment needs to incorporate three lines, based largely on the preceding social phobia package. First, you will need to discuss with your client the motivations for her actions as well as the consequences. A discussion of self-handicapping, pointing out its inherent fallacy can be very useful. The disadvantages of self-handicapping/procrastination should also be discussed (i.e., it often produces behaviors that result in failure or not doing as well as you could have and ultimately lowers self-esteem). Second, the client needs to engage in standard cognitive restructuring for the beliefs underlying the procrastination. As described above, this will frequently relate to perfectionistic beliefs (e.g., "I must do this perfectly" or "I cannot make a mistake") based on a concern about negative evaluation. Finally, the client needs to incorporate these situations into her exposure hierarchy. Again, the exposure will generally be aimed at the issue of perfectionism. Therefore, clients will need to practice not doing things perfectly or at least taking chances in situations where they cannot assure a perfect outcome. This can include a wide variety of possibilities from not keeping the house perfectly clean, to not dressing in a completely coordinated manner, to intentionally putting an occasional error into a piece of work, and so on. Focusing on the realistic consequences of not being perfect in any of these situations is important. It is especially important to reduce perfectionism because it is often a compensation for a client's negative feelings about herself. Learning to accept both negative and positive aspects of oneself is an important step in raising self-esteem.

It is also a good idea to provide your client with some simple instructions in time management. Many clients who procrastinate are very disorganized. Often this is a result of perfectionism, which has so interfered with completing tasks that procrastination has become a way of life, contributing to a disorganized and overwhelming environment. A few weeks of carefully organized time tabling can act as a type of exposure exercise in itself, demonstrating to clients that structuring time and getting tasks completed is not as difficult or as bad as they feared. We do not have space in this book to discuss time management in detail, but several good books exist (e.g., Lakein 1973).

ISSUES TO DO WITH TRUST

If you deal with people diagnosed with social phobia, you will eventually have to confront issues of trust. This is especially the case for people who meet criteria for avoidant personality disorder. One of the criteria for this disorder is an unwillingness to get involved with others unless certain of being liked, a clear indication of lack of trust. Indeed, people with social phobia see others as highly critical.

Trust is the expectancy that most people will not intentionally hurt our feelings. In cognitive terms, we could say that it is an expectancy that the probability of being emotionally hurt by another person is low. Further, for most people there is a willingness to exercise that expectancy because there is also a belief that the consequences of being hurt are not tragic. Most people believe that if they are emotionally hurt by another they have the personal resources to overcome it, and that getting hurt from time to time is a normal part of life and not a sign of one's inherent defects.

People who have difficulties with trust do not share these beliefs. In most situations they will entertain a high probability that others will hurt them. As a result, they will require more explicit evidence against this eventuality than will most others, often an unrealistic amount. In addition, these individuals are likely to doubt that they have the personal resources to cope with hurt. Therefore, there will often be an underlying belief along the lines "I should never feel any emotional pain." This belief is preserved because they spend their lives avoiding the possibility of emotional pain and they never learn that they can cope with it if it does occur.

Changing such beliefs is a very difficult task, largely because it is difficult to obtain clear evidence to the contrary. In addition, these beliefs are usually very entrenched and, by their very nature, don't allow the kind of tests that would provide contradictory evidence.

If you have a client who has major difficulties with trust, it is very unlikely that you can expect to see marked changes within the usual time frame. Each step will, by necessity, be slow and painstaking. Steps will need to be small, first because evidence will often be misinterpreted to be consistent with her belief, and second, because any experience interpreted as negative can cause the client to drop out of treatment.

The first step in treatment must be to model trust within the therapeutic relationship. Obviously, you will need to adhere more strongly than ever to the usual therapeutic rules of honesty and integrity. Remember that quite innocent oversights or withheld information can be misinterpreted as an intentional slight. Even constructive criticism in the context of therapy may be seen as supporting the idea that others are critical. You will probably find that you need to be somewhat more open and sharing of your own personal life than you might otherwise be. It is especially helpful to share some of your personal weaknesses, showing your client that you are not perfect either. In addition, it will be very useful to explicitly discuss some of the general ground rules of therapy, such as confidentiality. Clients with extreme lack of trust may find group situations too difficult to participate in.

The therapeutic situation can also be used to practice small steps in extending trust. You will often find that the client who has difficulty with trust will withhold information in therapy and will be reluctant to discuss certain topics. This is due to beliefs that you may use this information against her, that you may reject her, or that you may think negatively about her. It is important to address this issue directly with the client, raising her potential concerns, and discussing why they are highly unlikely. You will also need to gently explore whether there may be issues or facts that the client is withholding from you due to such concerns. In cases where this is found or suspected, it is a good idea to conceptualize it as a specific feared event. You should begin by applying cognitive restructuring to the situation of sharing this information with the therapist. That is, what does she think will happen if she shares this information with you, how likely is that, what is the consequence, and so on. Next, you need to engage in small exposure steps. The client needs to be encouraged to begin to share small pieces of personal information and then you need to stop and examine the consequences. It is important not to pressure the client too much with respect to sharing, especially early in therapy. However, this gentle approach needs to be balanced with encouragement to the client to begin to disclose small amounts of information. Even after this is done, it will be important to check with her from time to time about whether there are issues that she is still unwilling to share.

It may also be valuable to spend some time helping the client develop insight. Discussion of family of origin, messages from parents and significant others, important experiences in life, and so on, can often be revealing. Helping the client to identify the sources of her beliefs may help to put them into a context and provide a sensible rationale for why she thinks the way she does. For example, a client who was always criticized by her mother throughout childhood may have developed a self-critical thinking style that she then carried into adulthood, leading to social fears. When the sources of negative self beliefs are uncovered you can go further to help the client restructure her view of these messages. For example, a client might relate how her father left the family when she was young and she has blamed herself and believed that all relationships are fragile since that time. This can lead to a discussion of the type of man her father was and the relationship difficulties her parents had and, through the use of evidence, lead her to a realization that this is not necessarily the blueprint for all relationships. Since the thinking styles a client has are probably related to prior experiences, this gives the therapist an opportunity to link the past with the present. It is most important to focus on modifying the cognitive style in the present, rather than focusing extensively on the past.

Finally, the usual cognitive restructuring and exposure must also be applied to *in vivo* trust situations. As mentioned earlier, these exercises will need to be taken slowly and, at first, at a pace where the client is not overwhelmed with anxiety. The client should be encouraged to have a trust hierarchy where gradually increasing efforts are made to be more and more open and trusting of others. For example, she may begin with exercises as simple as "telling a stranger her name," or "smiling at a colleague." Later she may do things such as "inviting a colleague out for a drink," or "discussing personal issues with a friend." Such exercises would generally be accompanied by discussions of appropriateness and social expectations. It is particularly important to address perfectionistic standards here, wherein the client believes that if she does not measure up in some way, others will think negatively of her.

11

✍

Termination

AIMS

1. Reviewing treatment techniques and applications.
2. Discussing treatment progress.
3. Discussing possible relapse and future practice.

Review of Treatment Techniques

By now you have covered with your client all of the new information and all of the techniques that he will need. From here, the key to making lasting behavioral changes is *practice*. At this point, it is often a valuable task to provide a brief synopsis of the treatment techniques, their mode of practice, and their application. You should go through each of the techniques in turn and briefly review the rationale for the technique and the method of practicing the procedure, from basics through to shortcuts. You may then wish to discuss a few examples with your client of ways of applying the procedure. It is a good idea to audiotape this session so the client can listen to it in the future.

Given that treatment to this point has focused on each technique in isolation, a particularly valuable exercise is to discuss ways of putting the treatment techniques together. You should point out to your client that he now has an armament of coping skills rather than a set of isolated procedures. It may be useful to discuss with him the similarities and differences among the procedures and how they can fit together and complement each other. Specifically, it is a good idea to provide a hypothetical situation and discuss how the client might approach it using the full range of techniques.

For example, you might suggest to your client that he imagine applying for a new job. One day the phone rings and he is invited to an interview in one week's time, in front of a panel of four managers. How might he prepare for and handle such a stressor? Discussion would then focus on the following: (1) use of cognitive restructuring to reduce the anticipatory anxiety. In particular, given the high threat of this situation, it may be valuable to go back to basics and use the monitoring forms to write out all of the beliefs and their challenges. This can then be used as a daily reminder of the realistic approach to the situation. (2) If there is particular anxiety over the situation, it may be valuable to develop a hierarchy of similar situations (e.g., telling a joke to a small group, giving a formal presentation to a group, doing a practice interview with colleagues), and to practice them over the coming week. (3) These practice situations, especially the role play with colleagues, can serve to provide feedback about performance and ways of improving it. Videoing may be useful, and so is honest, constructive feedback from colleagues. (4) In the final interview the client needs to remember to focus attention on the questions and his answers rather than on negative thoughts or the imagined negative thoughts of the interviewers. In the week leading up to the interview, the client may want to practice attention-focusing exercises and should also take the opportunity to practice focusing attention during the role play. (5) The client can do several imaginal exposure exercises focusing on details of past job interviews and/or conjuring up an image of the forthcoming interview. (6) Finally, the client needs to remind himself that sitting in a competitive interview is threatening for anyone and that some degree of anxiety is natural, expected, and quite realistic. Expecting to be completely relaxed will only heighten the client's fear. Overall and realistically, the client's newly learned skills should help to reduce the anxiety but will not eliminate it.

Treatment Progress

The second aim of this final session is to review the gains and progress your client has made throughout the program. Hopefully, these gains will be obvious and your client will be satisfied with the changes he has made. However, treatment progress rarely occurs in a smooth and consistent fashion and both you and your client need to remind yourselves of this. It is just as easy for therapists to become disheartened with treatment as it is for clients. Nevertheless, your task is to keep your client enthused and motivated to continue to apply the treatment techniques and to keep practicing. For the first year or so, the client needs to make these techniques a part of his life. Providing a review of treatment progress is an excellent way to increase the motivation to keep practicing. In addition, being realistic about the chances of relapse will highlight the importance of continuing to practice the elements of the program.

A common feature in treatment of any disorder is a shift in the goals and expected outcomes of therapy over time. When your client first presented for treatment, he may have been highly distressed and may have hoped for any degree of improvement. Over time, as improvement occurred, you may have found that the early distress was forgotten and the client set implicitly higher standards for his outcome goals. While this is not necessarily a bad thing, it is easy to become disheartened if he has forgotten the point from which he began. In this case it may seem as if there has been little if any gain. In such cases, it is very important to remind the client of how he presented and the initial goals of therapy. Simply getting your client to consciously recall his life several months ago, in particular focusing on concrete limitations, is generally sufficient. Going back over your intake notes can also help, as well as readministering some of the self-report measures of anxiety and comparing your client's later responses to his initial ones. Finally, it is very useful to ask your client to bring in his early monitoring forms. Once this initial baseline has been established, you are in a position to discuss the changes seen in therapy. Your client should be able to point out the concrete changes in behavior as well as changes in his feelings and attitudes toward social situations. In addition, you may wish to provide feedback on how he currently presents, contrasting this with his initial presentation, while at the same time empathizing with the client's desire to rid himself of distress. You may also wish to ask whether he has noticed others reacting to him in different ways or whether there have been any overt comments about changes. In this way, you can reinforce your client's faith in the value of the procedures, thereby increasing the likelihood that he will continue to use them.

Relapse Prevention and the Future

Following the discussion of treatment progress, you will want to move to a discussion of the future. The most likely scenario is that your client will have demonstrated solid gains but that further improvement can still be made. At this point, discussion of goals for the future is important, and it may be that the client will wish to set new goals other than those that were originally made. He may now be willing to consider addressing situations that were too threatening at the beginning of treatment. It is most important to emphasize the necessity of regular practice. The biggest danger is found with clients who make enough gains to overcome their initial crisis and, as a result, lose their motivation to practice and forge ahead. Clients need to be reminded that it is easy to slip back into old habits. You should set aside sufficient time to discuss a new set of goals for the future and the methods and techniques that could be used to achieve them.

An approximate timetable for achieving these goals can also he prevent the client from losing his way. Don't forget to record the goal. and methods and give a copy of them to the client.

Depending on financial and practical considerations, it may also be useful to arrange to continue to see your client beyond this point. These future treatment sessions would primarily be aimed at setting and discussing homework and dealing with any difficulties that might arise. Assuming that your client does not have any special needs, future sessions may be set biweekly, monthly, or even less frequently than that. It is best to taper sessions at this point, perhaps meeting once every other week for two sessions, then once per month for two sessions, and so on. This will allow your client to gain confidence in his ability to maintain progress without depending on you. As we discussed earlier, social situations are often difficult to arrange, so less frequent sessions will allow more time for practice. These infrequent sessions are still vitally important, however, because they provide the impetus for your client to continue practice. In addition to serving as a booster to reinforce skills, they also help to maintain the client's focus on the problem.

The final issue to discuss in the termination session is the possibility of relapse. Clients need to be informed that relapse is a frequent occurrence. Most important, however, they need to understand that relapse is not a terminal sentence. In fact, we often call it a "lapse" to suggest that it is temporary. The skills and techniques they have learned can never be taken away from them and, although they may stop using them for some reason, they can always reinstate them.

Relapse tends to occur either subtly or suddenly. Subtle relapse typically occurs because the client has stopped using his techniques and has failed to notice the signs of gradual loss of confidence. The importance of regular practice cannot be overstated. Clearly, it is unrealistic to expect the average client to engage in daily practice for the rest of his life. However, it may be useful for your client to schedule regular checks and practice periods into his life, at least the forseeable future. For example, he may decide to practice attentional training exercises daily for one week out of every two months. Similarly, he may at this time review the previous month and search for any instances of avoidance behavior that he engaged in. If avoidant behaviors and loss of confidence are beginning to creep back in, then reinstatement of practice of techniques for a brief period should help.

Sudden relapse is more likely to occur following a specific event. This may be a major life event, such as the death of a significant other or serious illness, or may be a slightly less severe but still confidence-sapping stressor such as the break-up of a relationship or loss of a job. The key is mental preparation. As long as the client realizes what is happening and the cause of his reduced confidence, adjustment can be made. The danger is that the client does not connect his reduced confidence with the stressor and begins to become depressed and amotivational over this seeming additional problem. If a major stressor is experienced, the client needs to first understand that his loss of confidence is an expected reaction to the stressor and that it will return to some extent with time. Second, he needs to return to basics for several weeks. That is, he needs to recommence monitoring, reinstate basic practice of techniques (e.g., use of cognitive restructuring forms), and reintroduce practice exercises (e.g., exposure hierarchies). Assuming the problem is caught early enough, improvement should be rapid.

DIFFICULT CLIENTS

A small proportion of clients will show little or no improvement following the treatment program. For your own mental health, it is important to remember that we all have treatment failures and, ultimately, it is the client's responsibility whether to adopt the techniques he has been taught. Nevertheless, a failure to improve may be a signal to you that alternative factors need to be taken into account.

There are many idiosyncratic reasons for lack of improvement and the therapist's main task is to try to identify the reason(s) that the particular client failed to respond. You should conduct a functional analysis of the presenting problem (ideally, this should have been done at the beginning of treatment anyway) and consider a variety of alternative conceptualizations to your original one. Might there be additional factors maintaining the problem? Might the presenting problem not be the real issue or the most important problem? Might there be additional factors complicating the overall picture? Comorbidity is a common complication. People with social phobia frequently also meet criteria for major depression or alcohol abuse. While you may have made a decision to treat the social phobia first, you might now consider, in hindsight, whether a comorbid condition could have interfered with treatment response. If additional factors are interfering with motivation to change (e.g., if the client is being supported or reinforced for his behavior) it may be important to go over the motivational procedures such as discussing the limitations on current lifestyle caused by social phobia and the benefits of not fearing social situations. In addition, it may be necessary to include other family members in treatment, especially if these members have been undermining treatment progress. At this point, considering other possible treatment approaches may be reasonable.

CONCLUSION

You may have begun this book as a relative novice in the treatment of people with social phobia. If so, you may have treated one or more people with this problem by now, using the guidelines suggested in the program. Alternately, you may have picked up this book as a therapist who is experienced with this population. In this case, we hope that the book has provided some new insights and additional ideas to complement your experience. In either case, you will have found along the way that applying a manualized therapy, such as the one presented here, is neither straightforward, nor mechanistic. Each client is a unique individual and requires a carefully tailored and finely adjusted program. In addition, as we discussed at the outset, the client–therapist relationship is vital in the optimum delivery of treatment, especially for this population. It is hoped that you have found the program laid out in this book to complement and extend your natural therapeutic style, rather than experiencing it as a constraint. As you gain more experience with this program, you will find yourself freeing up to incorporate more and more of your own personal style into your delivery.

People with social phobia are a rewarding population to work with. They are generally pleasant, highly motivated, and provide many complex challenges to the therapist. They do not respond to treatment with complete ease, yet at the same time, they generally show significant and concrete gains following a treatment program such as the one described here. We hope that your client was able to benefit from this treatment and that you have been encouraged to continue to incorporate these techniques into your repertoire.

৵ References ৵

Agras, W. S., Leitenberg, H., and Barlow, D. H. (1968). Social rein-
forcement in the modification of agoraphobia. *Archives of General Psychiatry* 19:423–427.

Andrews, G. (1996). Comorbidity in neurotic disorders: the similarities are more important than the differences. In *Current Controversies in the Anxiety Disorders*, ed. R. M. Rapee, pp. 3–20.
New York: Guilford.

Asmundson, G. J. G., and Stein, M. B. (1994). Selective processing
of social threat in patients with generalized social phobia: evaluation using a dot-probe paradigm. *Journal of Anxiety Disorders*
8:107–117.

Barlow, D. H. (1988). *Anxiety and Its Disorders: The Nature and
Treatment of Anxiety and Panic*. New York: Guilford.

Beck, A. T., Emery, G., and Greenberg, R. L. (1985). *Anxiety Disorders and Phobias: A Cognitive Perspective*. New York: Basic Books.

Beck, A. T., Epstein, N., Brown, G., and Steer, R. A. (1989). An
inventory for measuring clinical anxiety: psychometric properties. *Journal of Consulting and Clinical Psychology* 56:893–897.

Beck, A. T., Ward, C. H., Mendelsohn, M., et al. (1961). An inventory for measuring depression. *Archives of General Psychiatry*
4:561–571.

Benson, H. (1976). *The Relaxation Response*. Boston: G. K. Hall.

Brown, E. J., Heimberg, R. G., and Juster, H. R. (1995). Social phobia
subtype and avoidant personality disorder: effect on severity of
social phobia, impairment, and outcome of cognitive-behavioral
treatment. *Behavior Therapy* 26:467–486.

Burns, D. D. (1985). *Intimate Connections: The Clinically Proven Program for Making Friends and Finding a Loving Partner*. New York: Morrow.

Butler, G., and Mathews, A. (1983). Cognitive processes in anxiety. *Advances in Behaviour Research and Therapy* 5:51–62.

Caspi, A., Elder, G. H.,Jr., and Bem, D. J. (1988). Moving away from the world: life-course patterns of shy children. *Developmental Psychology* 24:824–831.

Chambless, D. L. (1990). Spacing of exposure sessions in treatment of agoraphobia and simple phobia. *Behavior Therapy* 21:217–229.

Chambless, D. L., Foa, E. B., Groves, G. A., and Goldstein, A. J. (1982). Exposure and communications training in the treatment of agoraphobia. *Behaviour Research and Therapy* 20:219–231.

Craske, M. G., Street, L., and Barlow, D. H. (1989). Instructions to focus upon or distract from internal cues during exposure treatment of agoraphobia avoidance. *Behaviour Research and Therapy* 27:663–672.

Dalgleish, T., and Watts, F. N. (1990). Biases of attention and memory in disorders of anxiety and depression. *Clinical Psychology Review* 10:589–604.

Di Nardo, P. A., Moras, K., Barlow, D. H., et al. (1993). Reliability of *DSM-III-R* anxiety disorder categories using the Anxiety Disorders Interview Schedule-Revised (ADIS-R). *Archives of General Psychiatry* 50:251–256.

Ellis, A., and Harper, R. A. (1975). *A New Guide to Rational Living*. Englewood Cliffs, NJ: Prentice Hall.

Emmelkamp, P. M. G., and Wessels, H. (1975). Flooding imagination vs flooding in vivo: a comparison with agoraphobics. *Behaviour Research and Therapy* 13:7–15.

Eysenck, M. W., Mogg, K., May, J., et al. (1991). Bias in interpretation of ambiguous sentences related to threat in anxiety. *Journal of Abnormal Psychology* 100:144–150.

Feske, U., and Chambless, D. L. (1995). Cognitive behavioral versus exposure only treatment for social phobia: a meta-analysis. *Behavior Therapy* 26:695–720.

Foa, E. B., Franklin, M. E., Perry, K. J., and Herbert, J. D. (1996). Cognitive biases in social phobia. *Journal of Abnormal Psychology* 105:433–439.

Foa, E. B., and McNally, R. J. (1996). Mechanisms of change in exposure therapy. In *Current Controversies in the Anxiety Disorders*, ed. R. M. Rapee, pp. 327–341. New York: Guilford.

Gelder, M. G., Bancroft, J. H. J., Gath, D. H., et al. (1973). Specific and non-specific factors in behavior therapy. *British Journal of Psychiatry* 123:445–462.

Ghosh, A., and Marks, I. M. (1987). Self-treatment of agoraphobia by exposure. *Behavior Therapy* 18:3–16.

Hargie, O., Saunders, C., and Dickson, D. (1994). *Social Skills in Interpersonal Communication* (3rd. ed.). New York: Routledge.

Heimberg, R. G., Dodge, C. S., Hope, D. A., et al. (1990). Cognitive behavioral group treatment for social phobia: comparison with a credible placebo control. *Cognitive Therapy and Research* 14:1–23.

Heimberg, R. G., Hope, D. A., Rapee, R. M., and Bruch, M. A. (1988). The validity of the Social Avoidance and Distress Scale and the Fear of Negative Evaluation Scale with social phobic patients. *Behaviour Research and Therapy* 26:407–410.

Heimberg, R. G., and Juster, H. R. (1995). Cognitive-behavioral treatments: literature review. In *Social Phobia: Diagnosis, Assessment, and Treatment*, ed. R. G. Heimberg, M. R. Liebowitz, D. A. Hope, and F. R. Schneier, pp. 261–309. New York: Guilford.

Heimberg, R. G., Liebowitz, M. R., Hope, D. A., et al. (1997). *Cognitive-behavioral group therapy versus phenelzine in the treatment of social phobia: I. 12-week outcome.* Manuscript submitted for publication.

Herbert, J. D., Hope, D. A., and Bellack, A. S. (1992). Validity of the distinction between generalized social phobia and avoidant personality disorder. *Journal of Abnormal Psychology* 101:332–339.

Hudson, J. L., and Rapee, R. M. (in press). The origins of social phobia. *Behavior Modification*.

Kessler, R. C., McGonagle, K. A., Zhao, S., et al. (1994). Lifetime and 12-month prevalence of *DSM-III-R* psychiatric disorders in the United States: results from the national comorbidity survey. *Archives of General Psychiatry* 51:8–19.

Lakein, A. (1973). *How To Get Control of Your Time and Your Life*. New York: Signet.

Lange, A. J., and Jakubowski, P. (1976). *Responsible Assertive Behavior: Cognitive/Behavioral Procedures for Trainers*. Champaign, IL: Research Press.

Leary, M. R. (1983). A brief version of the Fear of Negative Evaluation Scale. *Personality and Social Psychology Bulletin* 9:371–375.

Liebowitz, M. R., Heimberg, R. G., et al. *Cognitive-behavioral group therapy versus phenelzine in social phobia: II. Long-term outcome*. Manuscript submitted for publication.

Lucock, M. P., and Salkovskis, P. M. (1988). Cognitive factors in social anxiety and its treatment. *Behaviour Research and Therapy* 26:297–302.

Mattick, R. P., Peters, L., and Clarke, J. C. (1989). Exposure and cognitive restructuring for social phobia: a controlled study. *Behavior Therapy* 20:3–23.

Meichenbaum, D. (1977). *Cognitive-Behavior Modification: An Integrative Approach*. New York: Plenum.

Norton, G. R., McLeod, L., Guertin, J., et al. (1996). Panic disorder or social phobia: Which is worse? *Behaviour Research and Therapy* 34:273–276.

Paul, G. L. (1966). *Insight Versus Desensitization in Psychotherapy*. Stanford, CA: Stanford University Press.

Rachman, S., Craske, M., Tallman, K., and Solyom, C. (1986). Does escape behavior strengthen agoraphobic avoidance?: a replication. *Behavior Therapy* 17:366–384.

Rapee, R. M. (1995). Descriptive psychopathology of social phobia. In *Social Phobia: Diagnosis, Assessment, and Treatment*, ed.

R. G. Heimberg, M. R. Liebowitz, D. A. Hope, and F. R. Schneier, pp. 41–66. New York: Guilford.

——— (1997). Potential role of childrearing practices in the development of anxiety and depression. *Clinical Psychology Review* 17.

——— (1998). *Overcoming Shyness and Social Phobia: A Step-by-Step Guide.* Northvale, NJ: Jason Aronson.

Rapee, R. M., Craske, M. G., and Barlow, D. H. (1994). Assessment instrument for panic disorder that includes fear of sensation-producing activities: The Albany Panic and Phobia Questionnaire. *Anxiety* 1:114–122.

Rapee, R. M., and Hayman, K. (1996). The effects of video feedback on the self-evaluation of performance in socially anxious subjects. *Behaviour Research and Therapy* 34:315–322.

Rapee, R. M., and Heimberg, R. G. (1997). A cognitive-behavioural model of anxiety in social phobia. *Behaviour Research and Therapy* 35:741–756.

Rapee, R. M., and Lim, L. (1992). Discrepancy between self and observer ratings of performance in social phobics. *Journal of Abnormal Psychology* 101:727–731.

Rapee, R. M., McCallum, S. L., Melville, L. F., et al. (1993). Memory bias in social phobia. *Behaviour Research and Therapy* 32:89–99.

Rathus, S. A. (1973). A 30-item schedule for assessing assertive behavior. *Behavior Therapy* 4:398–406.

Ribordy, S. C., Tracy, R. J., and Bernotas, T. D. (1981). The effects of an attentional training procedure on the performance of high and low test-anxious children. *Cognitive Therapy and Research* 5:19–28.

Sanderson, W. C., Di Nardo, P. A., Rapee, R. M., and Barlow, D. H. (1990). Syndrome co-morbidity in patients diagnosed with a *DSM-III-Revised* anxiety disorder. *Journal of Abnormal Psychology* 99:308–312.

Sanderson, W. C., and McGinn, L. K. (1997). Psychotherapy for anxiety disorder patients with psychiatric comorbidity. In *Treatment Strategies for Patients with Psychiatric Comorbidity*, ed. S. Wetzler and W. C. Sanderson, pp. 75–104. New York: Wiley.

Schneier, F. R., Johnson, J., Hornig, C. D., et al. (1992). Social phobia: comorbidity and morbidity in an epidemiologic sample. *Archives of General Psychiatry* 49:282–288.

Selzer, M. L., Vinokur, A., and van Rooijen, L. (1975). A self-administered short Michigan Alcoholism Screening Test (SMAST). *Journal of Studies on Alcohol* 36:117–126.

Snyder, C. R., and Smith, T. W. (1982). Symptoms as self-handicapping strategies: the virtues of old wine in a new bottle. In *Integrations of Clinical and Social Psychology*, ed. G. Weary and H. L. Mirels, pp. 104–127. New York: Oxford University Press.

Stravinsky, A., Lamontagne, Y., and Lavallee, Y. (1986). Clinical phobias and avoidant personality disorder among alcoholics admitted to an alcoholism rehabilitation setting. *Canadian Journal of Psychiatry* 31:714–719.

Suinn, R. M. (1969). The STABS, a measure of test anxiety for behavior therapy: normative data. *Behaviour Research and Therapy* 8:335–339.

Trower, P. (1986). Social skills training and social anxiety. In *Handbook of Social Skills Training*, ed. C. R. Holin and P. Trower. New York: Pergamon.

Turner, S. M., Beidel, D. C., Dancu, C. V., and Stanley, M. A. (1989). An empirically derived inventory to measure social fears and anxiety: the social phobia and anxiety inventory. *Psychological Assessment: A Journal of Consulting and Clinical Psychology* 1:35–40.

Turner, S. M., Beidel, D. C., and Townsley, R. M. (1990). Social phobia: relationship to shyness. *Behaviour Research and Therapy* 28:497–505.

Watson, D., and Friend, R. (1969). Measurement of social-evaluative anxiety. *Journal of Consulting and Clinical Psychology* 33:448–457.

Wells, J. E., Bushnell, J. A., Hornblow, A. R., et al. (1989). Christchurch psychiatric epidemiology study, part 1: methodology and lifetime prevalence for specific psychiatric disorders. *Australian and New Zealand Journal of Psychiatry* 23:315–326.

Wetzler, S., and Sanderson, W. C., eds. (1997). *Treatment Strategies for Patients with Psychiatric Comorbidity*. New York: Wiley.

Williams, S. L. (1996). Therapeutic changes in phobic behavior are mediated by changes in perceived self-efficacy. In *Current Controversies in the Anxiety Disorders*, ed. R. M. Rapee, pp. 344–368. New York: Guilford.

Wolpe, J. (1958). *Psychotherapy by Reciprocal Inhibition*. Stanford, CA: Stanford University Press.

Ziegler, S. G. (1994). The effects of attentional shift training on the execution of soccer skills: a preliminary investigation. *Journal of Applied Behavior Analysis* 27:545–552.

Zimbardo, P. G., Pilkonis, P. A., and Norwood, R. M. (1974). *The Silent Prison of Shyness*. Stanford, CA: Office of Naval Research Technical Report No. 2–17. Stanford University.

Suggested
ᔭ Further Readings ᔭ

NATURE AND DESCRIPTION OF SOCIAL PHOBIA

Beidel, D. C., Turner, S. M., and Dancu, C. V. (1985). Physiological, cognitive and behavioral aspects of social anxiety. *Behaviour Research and Therapy* 23:109–117.

Brooks, R. B., Baltazar, P. L., and Munjak, D. J. (1989). Co-occurrence of personality disorders with panic disorder, social phobia, and generalized anxiety disorder: a review of the literature. *Journal of Anxiety Disorders* 3:259–285.

Bruch, M. A., and Heimberg, R. G. (1994). Differences in perceptions of parental and personal characteristics between generalized and nongeneralized social phobics. *Journal of Anxiety Disorders* 8:155–168.

Heimberg, R. G. (1996). Social phobia, avoidant personality disorder, and the multiaxial conceptualization of interpersonal anxiety. In *Trends in Cognitive and Behavioural Therapies, vol. 1*, ed. P. Salkovskis, pp. 43–62. Sussex, England: Wiley.

Hope, D. A., and Heimberg, R. G. (1988). Public and private self-consciousness and social phobia. *Journal of Personality Assessment* 52:626–639.

Mannuzza, S., Fyer, A. J., Liebowitz, M. R., and Klein, D. F. (1990). Delineating the boundaries of social phobia: its relationship to panic disorder and agoraphobia. *Journal of Anxiety Disorders* 4:41–59.

Norton, G. R., McLeod, L., Guertin, J., et al.. (1996). Panic disorder or social phobia: Which is worse? *Behaviour Research and Therapy* 34:273–276.

Rapee, R. M. (1995). Descriptive psychopathology of social phobia. In *Social Phobia: Diagnosis, Assessment, and Treatment*, ed. R. G. Heimberg, M. R. Liebowitz, D. A. Hope, and F. R. Schneier, pp. 41–66. New York: Guilford.

Schneier, F. R., Johnson, J., Hornig, C. D., et al. (1992). Social phobia: comorbidity and morbidity in an epidemiologic sample. *Archives of General Psychiatry* 49:282–288.

Schneier, F. R., Martin, L. Y., Liebowitz, M. R., et al. (1989). Alcohol abuse in social phobia. *Journal of Anxiety Disorders* 3:15–23.

Turner, S. M., and Beidel, D. C. (1989). Social phobia: clinical syndrome, diagnosis, and comorbidity. *Clinical Psychology Review* 9:3–18.

Turner, S. M., Beidel, D. C., Dancu, C. V., and Keys, D. J. (1986). Psychopathology of social phobia and comparison to avoidant personality disorder. *Journal of Abnormal Psychology* 95:389–394.

Widiger, T. A. (1992). Generalized social phobia versus avoidant personality disorder: a commentary on three studies. *Journal of Abnormal Psychology* 101:340–343.

MODELS AND EXPERIMENTAL STUDIES OF SOCIAL PHOBIA

Alden, L. E., and Wallace, S. T. (1995). Social phobia and social appraisal in successful and unsuccessful social interactions. *Behaviour Research and Therapy* 33:497–506.

Asmundson, G. J. G., and Stein, M. B. (1994). Selective processing of social threat in patients with generalized social phobia: evaluation using a dot-probe paradigm. *Journal of Anxiety Disorders,* 8:107–117.

Bond, N. W., and Siddle, D. A. T. (1996). The preparedness account of social phobia: some data and alternative explanations. In *Current Controversies in the Anxiety Disorders*, ed. R. M. Rapee, pp. 291–314. New York: Guilford.

Bruch, M. A., and Cheek, J. M. (1995). Developmental factors in childhood and adolescent shyness. In *Social Phobia: Diagnosis, Assessment, and Treatment*, ed. R. G. Heimberg, M. R. Liebowitz, D. A. Hope, and F. R. Schneier, pp. 163–184. New York: Guilford.

Clark, D. M., and Wells, A. (1995). A cognitive model of social phobia. In *Social Phobia: Diagnosis, Assessment, and Treatment*, ed. R. G. Heimberg, M. R. Liebowitz, D. A. Hope, and F. R. Schneier, pp. 69–93. New York: Guilford.

Cloitre, M., Heimberg, R. G., Holt, C. S., and Liebowitz, M. R. (1992). Reaction time to threat stimuli in panic disorder and social phobia. *Behaviour Research and Therapy* 30:609–618.

Hudson, J. L., and Rapee, R. M. (in press). The origins of social phobia. *Behavior Modification*.

Levin, A. P., Schneier, F. R., and Liebowitz, M. R. (1989). Social phobia: biology and pharmacology. *Clinical Psychology Review* 9:129–140.

Mineka, S., and Zinbarg, R. (1995). Conditioning and ethological models of social phobia. In *Social Phobia: Diagnosis, Assessment, and Treatment*. ed. R. G. Heimberg, M. R. Liebowitz, D. A. Hope, and F. R. Schneier, pp. 134–162. New York: Guilford.

Plomin, R., and Daniels, D. (1986). Genetics and shyness. In *Shyness: Perspectives on Research and Treatment*, ed. W. H. Jones, J. M. Cheek, and S. R. Briggs, pp. 63–80. New York: Plenum.

Poulton, R. G., and Andrews, G. (1994). Appraisal of danger and proximity in social phobics. *Behaviour Research and Therapy* 32:639–642.

Rapee, R. M., and Heimberg, R. G. (1997). A cognitive-behavioural model of anxiety in social phobia. *Behaviour Research and Therapy* 35:741–756.

Rapee, R. M., McCallum, S. L., Melville, L. F., et al. (1993). Memory bias in social phobia. *Behaviour Research and Therapy* 32:89–99.

Strauman, T. J. (1989). Self-discrepancies in clinical depression and social phobia: Cognitive structures that underlie emotional disorders? *Journal of Abnormal Psychology* 98:14–22.

Wallace, S. T., and Alden, L. E. (1991). A comparison of social standards and perceived ability in anxious and nonanxious men. *Cognitive Therapy and Research* 15:237–254.

Winton, E. C., Clark, D. M., and Edelmann, R. J. (1995). Social anxiety, fear of negative evaluation and the detection of negative emotion in others. *Behaviour Research and Therapy* 33:193–196.

TREATMENT OF SOCIAL PHOBIA

Butler, G., Cullington, A., Munby, M., et al. (1984). Exposure and anxiety management in the treatment of social phobia. *Journal of Consulting and Clinical Psychology* 52:642–650.

Emmelkamp, P. M. G., Mersch, P., Vissia, E., and van der Helm, M. (1985). Social phobia: A comparative evaluation of cognitive and behavioral interventions. *Behaviour Research and Therapy* 23:365–369.

Feske, U., and Chambless, D. L. (1995). Cognitive behavioral versus exposure only treatment for social phobia: a meta-analysis. *Behavior Therapy* 26:695–720.

Heimberg, R. G., Dodge, C. S., Hope, D. A., et al. (1990). Cognitive behavioral group treatment for social phobia: comparison with a credible placebo control. *Cognitive Therapy and Research* 14:1–23.

Heimberg, R. G., and Juster, H. R. (1995). Cognitive-behavioral treatments: literature review. In *Social Phobia: Diagnosis, Assessment, and Treatment*, ed. R. G. Heimberg, M. R. Liebowitz, D. A. Hope, and F. R. Schneier, pp. 261–309. New York: Guilford.

Mattick, R. P., and Peters, L. (1988). Treatment of severe social phobia: effects of guided exposure with and without cognitive restructuring. *Journal of Consulting and Clinical Psychology* 56:251–260.

Scholing, A., and Emmelkamp, P. M. G. (1993). Exposure with and without cognitive therapy for generalized social phobia: effects of individual and group treatment. *Behaviour Research and Therapy* 31:667–681.

Turner, S. M., Beidel, D. C., Cooley, M. R., et al. (1994). A multicomponent behavioral treatment for social phobia: social effectiveness therapy. *Behaviour Research and Therapy* 32:381–390.

Turner, S. M., Beidel, D. C., and Cooley-Quille, M. R. (1995). Two-year follow-up of social phobics treated with Social Effectiveness Therapy. *Behaviour Research and Therapy* 33:553–556.

ᔍ Index ᔍ